BLACK COUNTRY FOLK AT WERK

NED WILLIAMS

Henry Thomas	Elizabeth Stead
Ronald Adams	Tom Millington
Archie Williams	Harold Fletcher
Syd Darby	Albert Clarke
Jim Dacre	Geoff Stevens
Harry Butler	Malcolm Palmer
Leslie Browne	Edna Vaughn
George Dorsett	Joan Powderly
George Edwards	Cyril Lord
Ted Green	John Downs
Cecil Westwood	Haydn Smith
Archie Clarke	Betty Crump
Malcolm Timmins	Alex Chatwin
Dot Davies	Charles Dickinson
Emma Whyle	Reg Share
Dennis Barnsley	Jack Griffiths
Lucy Woodhall	Alan Butler
Ralph Smith	Vera Taylor
Sid Wooldridge	Harry Tonks
Cyril Harper	Margaret Davies
John & Eunice Horton	Donald Blytheway
Charlie Price	Lucy Price
Ron Hawkins	Ken Grainger
Jack Halksworth	Audrey Grainger
Freda Shaw	Marjorie Bowman
Joyce Olvier	Bernadette Elwell
Howard Freeman	Fred Onions

URALIA PRESS

23 WESTLAND ROAD   WOLVERHAMPTON WV3 9NZ

Above: Black Country Folk at Werk - from shinglers to shorthand typists.
Cover photo: Dennis Barnsley makin' chains, bent over the block in his
ganzey, providing him with some protection from the hot sparks.
(Photo: Dave Whyley)

Black Country Folk at Werk
Ned Williams
Uralia Press 1989

ISBN 0 9511223 3 9

Design: John Revill
Photo printing: Jan Endean
Photo screening: Brian Homer with Andy and Charlotte

Printed in the Black Country by
Gibbons Barford Print, Wolverhampton

CONTENTS

INTRODUCTION

As a teenager I was fascinated by the title of George Gurdjieff's book, "Meetings With Remarkble Men." It conjured up a picture of being a writer with nothing to do but sit at the feet of other people, being informed, entertained or inspired. Thirty years later I have at last been able to go through that experience, and produce this book as the result. Partly, however, this book has been produced to rectify past error! Whilst producing books on various aspects of local history for the past twenty years, I now realise that I have picked the brains of hundreds of local people in the quest for information and facts, of which I made many notes, but I have never recorded the actual words spoken to me. I have busily re-distributed information without ever letting the informants speak for themselves. In this book I hope to put that right.

A small select range of Black Country folk's autobiographical writing cconcerning the subject of work has been available for some time, and in recent years this has grown. Using the words of ordinary people, as opposed to academics and professional writers, to create a complex picture of peoples' working lives is not a new idea. Once again if I think back to my youth, I was brought up on the wonderful work of Ewan McColl and Charles Parker, creating the classic radio-ballads like "The Ballad of John Axon" - inspiring a generation of television documentarists like Philip Donellen ("Joe the Chain Maker").The concept of "oral history" has also developed and various local heritage projects and history groups have contributed to this in a valuable but piecemeal way. I do not think anybody has yet tried to make a definitive list of what has been done in this line.

Here at Uralia Press my first venture into publishing a Blackcountryman's account of his working life came in 1977 with the publication of John Hubbard's "No Steam Without Fire". It made me think it would be worth trying to record the story of Stafford Road Works in the words of the people who had worked there, but I was defeated by the magnitude of the project, and my own lack of experience in making recordings.

In recent years a number of local history publications have become obsessed with pictures. Whilst pictures are a very effective means of evoking the past, many of the pictures, which come from local library collections, are less ephemeral than the voices and memories of the people in the pictures! It would seem, therefore, that we have reached the point where

The ideal photograph of someone at work should show the individual concerned, the nature of the task andsomething of the environment, equipment etc..... as in this 1954 study of Wilfred Dunn at work. (BCS collection)

peoples' memories need preserving, in their own words, accompanied where possible with appropriate pictures. If these words are not collected future generations will look at our photo-album approach to local history and wonder why on earth we didn't take more care to identify the people in the photos ask them to say something while we had the chance! We have to start somewhere, so lets start by sharing memories of work. (This is spelt "werk" in the title in recognition of the fact that the word is given special attention in local dialects.)

If you ask chaps and wenches to share their experience of work with you, the subject oftens excites some initial antipathy. ("Geroff! - I try and forget work - don't ask me to talk about it.") But as you will see from the accounts presented in this book, many people not only enjoyed their work, but also excel in sharing the memory of it! I have known folks who are totally inarticulate about anything other than recent soap operas suddenly become remarkably eloquent on the subject of work, and the chief pleasure in creating this book has been to witness the enthusiasm people can have for talking about their jobs, whatever that job might be. Although work has consumed a vast quantity of these peoples' lives, and in many instances has had an adverse effect on these lives, you will see that most folk feel very positive about it. Cynically you could point to the two Bilston Steelworkers who are talking about their work in the present tense rather than as a "memory", and say that their feelings about work seem different. Against that it must be noted that several accounts are by people who have carried on working past retirement age in order to share their love of their work with others, for example Jack Halksworth of the Leather Centre and Tom Millington of the Lock Museum. As you will see, these people do not look back on work with rose tinted spectacles, but nevertheless they feel positive about it.

*These men are furnacemen, photographed at BSC Bilston
Steelworks in 1976. In a large Black Country Steelworks it
was possible to find people working there whose family had
worked there beforehand perhaps through three generations.
But in the middle of a large industrial conurbation a workforce is equally likely to consist of newcomers — people who
become "Black Country Folk" in order to work here and then
become part of the ever changing community, and that is
what makes them Black Country citizens — not their family
history, birthplace or colour of skin.*
(Nick Hedges)

What about the pictures? Although people can often
show you pictures of their weddings and their holidays, relatively few can show you pictures of their
work! There are interesting exceptions, and some of
those exceptions have found their way into this book.
The perfect picture should show us the individual concerned, something of the work undertaken, and something of the environment in which the work takes
place. No wonder such pictures are rare - it is easier
to snap Dad building a sandcastle on the beach than
it is to snap him tapping a furnace in some dark
satanic mill!

Instead we often have to make do with a nostalgic
view of the annual Works outing, or a "group portrait"
of the workforce, or views of retirement presentations.
All these are valuable but I have tried to find photographs for this book that are closer to the work itself.
Two other sources exist. The first of these is the "official photograph" commissioned by the employer. They
are the work of professional photographers able to
overcome some of the problems of taking photographs
in the work environment. The second source is the
person who sees work as a suitable subject for photo-
graphy, just as others like to photograph wildlife, railway engines, or photographic models.

In the light of these remarks it is important to draw

readers' attention to the fact that work in the Black
Country has already been presented in a book of
photographs and words. I refer to Nick Hedges' and
Huw Beynon's "Born to Work" (Pluto Press, 1982).
Local peoples' feelings and ideas about their work in
that book are used to present a rather sociological
view of the subject. Here people's words are presented
in a less digested form - and you are left to draw your
own conclusions. But if you are wondering how to
take pictures of work, Nick Hedges' pictures might
inspire you.

Having thought about photographs, what about the
words? A number of contributors to this book wrote
their accounts of their work. Many others chose to be
tape-recorded and have their words transcribed, but
it is not a literal transcption that appears here. In
nearly all cases I have edited, reshuffled and reor-
ganised the words and therefore I must take responsibility for what has arrived on the printed page. I
have tried to be faithful to the letter and the spirit of
the words I have been entrusted with, but if something
offends you may have to blame the editor rather than
the contributor. I also take blame or credit for what
I have chosen to include. I have tried to play down
my own interests in transport, cinemas, and retailing,
in order to try and achieve a reasonable cross-section

These girls were machinists (on slotting, shearing and blanking machines) at Sankey's Top Works, Bilston about 1937. Only the three on the right have been identified so far — from right to left: Poppy Gumrey, Rene Hawthorn and Joan Smith. In the Black Country there has been a long tradition of woman forming a large part of the labour force — and there has been an attempt to reflect this in the compilation of this book. (Wolverhampton Public Libraries)

of Black Country work-activity from a variety of criteria: geographical, occupational, social.

My definition of the Black Country is broad but I have tried to give mining and metal-working their rightful prominence. As we move into transport and service industries I have encouraged contributors to show how those jobs take on a Black Country flavour. The difficulty is not only to take a broad view, but also a long view, and one day the silicon chip might seem as important in the history of the Black Country as the Thirty Foot Seam and the foundry stack. In just over fifty accounts of peoples' work we can barely scratch the surface - I know your favourite workplace or occupation has probably been left out, but hopefully, with your help, that can be put right in subsequent volumes, or volumes devoted to single communities or particular groups of occupations.

Now for some conclusions on a serious note. Whilst working on this project I felt very conscious of three "shadows" hovering around the subject, and three "sources of light". The shadows are War, Unemployment, and Social & Economic Injustice. In many of these accounts you will see how the two World Wars intruded across local peoples' working lives. Unemployment also casts a long shadow. A popular view of Black Country History sees the region relatively stable and prosperous as a result of diversification that took place in the 1880s. Both statistics and individual experience present a rather different picture and unemployment is often mentioned in this book. Injustice exists in many forms and in these accounts there are details of poor financial reward, cruel termination of employment and miserable working conditions. Discrimination on the grounds of race, gender, and age and physical handicap lurks throughout the local world of work.

If you find such things too depressing or politically sensitive or just plain boring, you will be more heartened by the positve aspects of the accounts that follow. These aspects are; the willingness of people to share experience, the postitive attitudes and enthusiasm they have brought to the task, and lastly a Black Country sense of local community and comradeship that exists in the world of work, as in other aspects of peoples' lives.

I hope you enjoy reading these accounts of peoples' work as much as I have enjoyed collecting them.

Ned Williams
Wolverhampton 1989.

Acknowledgements

Obviously I would like to thank all the contributors to this book for their memories, their time and their generosity. The authorship of each account is clearly stated, and therefore I will not list them again here. Less obvious is the huge army of people who helped assemble the book in a variety of ways.

I would like to thank the following for "introductions", or pointing me in the right direction: Jim Evans, Tony Ball, Peter Eardley. Alton Douglas, Kath West. Some such people also conducted recordings for me: Denice Carter, David Watson, Jack Haddock, Dave Whyley, Ron Moss, April Garratt, Jane Vickers and Rosemary Morrell.

Many have helped in some "official" capacity: Liz Rees (Wolverhampton Archives), Alan Franklin (Bilston Library), John Maddison (Sandwell Local History Centre), the Walsall Local History Centre, Willenhall Lock Museum, Walsall Leather Centre. Photographic help has come from the local papers and the Black Country Bugle. Also from Nick Hedges, and from Keith Hodgkins and Dave Whyley of the Black Country Society. Two Wulfrun College students have also undertaken photographic assignments for the book: Anita Mehtra and Sarah Wood. Valuable keyboard advice came from James Quirke. Many other people have made contributions that hopefully will see the light of day in Volume Two!

At the production stage I have been assisted by Jan Endean who has worked on virtually all the photographs, by JJT Services for some prompt proof reading, and by John Revill for designing the book and preparing it to go to press.

REGISTERED   TRADE MARK

A photograph taken at Conex Sanbra, Tipton in 1951 of an unidentified machinist at work, a portrait of the subtle relationship between worker and machine. Is she reflecting on such matters? - or thinking of the financial rewards of piece work? - or dreaming of future automation, robotics and microelectronics? (BCS collection)

8

1

GETTING THE COAL

Above: Two miners at Baggeridge Colliery securing a hydraulic roof prop as the coalface advances in the early sixties. The Earl of Dudley's Baggeridge Colliery set out to reach the Thick Coal beyond the Western Boundary Fault, and borings began in 1896. The coal was found at a depth of six hundred yards. The size of the pit, and the depth at which the coal was found made the colliery rather different in character to the small pits associated with the Black Country, but because it survived until comparatively recent times it has served as a reminder to many local people of the area's identity in relation to coal. The pit produced coal from 1912 until 1967. Today, nearly quarter of a century later, only some temporary open-cast mining produces coal from the Black Country. Our identity as a coalfield is based on memories. (BCS Collection)

A Bevin Boy Meets Tommy

Henry Thomas

It was my first day down the mine. I hadn't got a clue what was going to happen. All I knew was that it was hole in the ground. We had to report to the Overman. That was the man who was in charge of the pit and who dished out the jobs. Of course the ordinary colliers went straight to the coalface, but we Bevin Boys had to get our orders from the Overman first. Well, you can imagine what I felt like when I got down there and he said,
"Yo'm used to 'orses ain't yer, bein' in the country?"
"Well", I said, "It's forty years since I've had anythin' to do with 'orses, but I know they've got a leg in each corner."
"Tek Tommy", he said, "An' go up the Burma Road."
"I doh know the road," I said. "'Ow'm I gonna gerrup there? I aven't gorra clue, me fust day down 'ere."
"E'll put yer right, do' worry. Just tell Tommy wheer yo' gorra go".
"Yo' pull the other one, mate," I replied.

It was a bewildering situation to be in and I thought perhaps he was pulling my leg, but one of the other men there said,
"Just tell 'im wheer yo' want to go, but keep up with 'im or yo'll get lost 'cos 'e'll be off."
And, do you know, Tommy was the most intelligent animal I've ever known in my life.

I took hold of the bridle. I wasn't going to let him lose me up the road because it was nearly a mile and a half to walk. I said, "Tommy! You've got to go to the Burma Road." and off he went up those narrow passages, in here, out there. He knew his way because he had been down the pit fourteen years. He was uncanny - I couldn't believe it - a horse with such sense. The blokes said, "Yo' needn't go with him every time."

Our job was to pull tubs of coal that miners had knocked out along the railway lines. There were other blokes whose job it was to take the full tubs off him and put two empty ones on. If those men weren't there he'd kick his chains off and come back.

The signals down the pit were just two wires, and you just put them together to ring the bell. One bell to start and three bells to stop. As soon as Tommy heard the one bell, off he'd go in the direction of the place I'd told him. But he wouldn't go if the points weren't set right. I think he could have done the job by himself. They said he knew more about the pit than anyone else. But he didn't know anything other than the pit because he never came out of it. He didn't know that there were grass fields or hedges up on the surface.

Five bells announced "snap" time, and the moment they went I put Tommy's corn down for his snap, but he wouldn't look at it! I wondered what was up with him. There were about twelve men at the coalface, squatting anywhere they could get comfortable, each having their lunch. Tommy walked up to the middle of them, and then went round the men just like a dog would at table. They gave him pieces of bread or bacon, and after they had all finished he went to his own snap, as if to say, "That's mine now!"

It was terrible down the pit with the dust, filth and grime, and the only drink you could have in the pit was what you brought down yourself. Bottles weren't allowed so you had to bring a tin can. I put my water down so that I'd know where to find it when I needed it, but when I did go to have a drink it had gone! I said to the blokes, "Have yo' drunk my water?" They said, "No - go and ask Tommy." I couldn't believe it.

A pit pony named Joey, at work at Baggeridge Colliery with Don Morris in 1967. In the small pits the ponies returned to the surface at the end of the shift, but at a large pit like Baggeridge they lived underground permanently. They worked one shift per day and were well looked after in the stables at the pit bottom. (BCS Collection)

Tommy had got the cork out of the can with his teeth, and lifted the bottle with his front legs and teeth and had drunk the lot! I went for my sandwiches, wrapped up in a hankerchief in my jacket pocket but Tommy had a marvellous sense of smell and had eaten his way straight through my pocket. The other blokes said, "Yo'll learn, yo'll learn with 'im."

It was very strange down the pit - I didn't know my way about at all. At about 2.15. eleven bells suddenly went - this was "knocking off time". Tommy turned round, knocked me out of the way, and was gone. I hadn't got a clue how to find my way out, and I had to wait for some blokes to come and show me the way. As I went by the stableman he asked me how I got on. He said, "Kid, he's got more brains than any bloke in the pit. I'm gonna tell you something - no leg pull - if ever Tommy stops, you stop. No matter where you are, if Tommy stops, you stop."

A time eventually arrived when I discovered the reason for this advice, and I shall never forget this for as long as I live. We had to go up to the Ridge in another part of the pit. Tommy knew the way and we were on one of the side roads when Tommy stopped. He wouldn't budge, so I rang the bell, as the nearest man was about a mile away. After a bit a miner came to investigate. He found that Tommy had heard the roof rumbling as some earth and rocks above us had moved. Tommy the pit pony could save your life!

Tommy was such a small pony you could lift him up. He was only about twice the size of an alsation dog, but he was very strong and tough and everybody thought the world of him. He used to pull two tubs along the rails. Each tub, when full, weighed half a ton. Some of the roads weren't very high and you had to bend to walk along them, sometimes for a mile at a time. Tommy could usually get through easily and you had a dickens of a job to keep up with him.

Some of the roads were on a steep slope. Sometimes tubs would get loose and come hurtling down the rails towards you. For this reason they cut out holes in the side of the roadway every now and then, so that if you heard a tub coming down you just about had time to dive into one of the safety holes. The trouble was that Tommy would be in there first! To this day I'm sure he laughed, as much to say, "Yo'm too late, mate! There's not enough room for you!" What an intelligent animal to find down that stinking cold bleak hole.

When I was due to be chucked out I went to the manager. "Mr. Nelson," I said, "Is there any chance of getting that pony and taking him home?"
"You can have him if you want, my lad", replied Billy Nelson. "He's due for coming out 'cos we're mechanised now and he's the last pony down the pit." I had to make lots of arrangements, including transport, though I suppose I could have taken him home on the bus - he was that small.

When I arrived to collect Tommy, the first thing they said was, "Don't be disappointed." He wasn't hurt but they had decided to bring in the vet to have a look at him. The vet said that the most humane thing would be to put him down because he didn't know what a green field was, and his eyes might have gone straight away after sixteen years down the pit. So they wouldn't let me have Tommy. They had shot him.

Jubilee

Ronald Adams

I went into the mines in 1943. Thirty of us had to go to a training pit at Nuneaton. We found ourselves sleeping in bunk beds in small rooms, and early the next morning the bus picked us up and away we went to Launchwood Pit. I felt very excited as we went into the cage and descended to the pit bottom. A lamp was fitted to our safety helmet, in an area that was still quite light, and the safety man took us on a tour of the pit for our first day.

We came to a big motor with a big wheel with a wire rope round it. This was called an endless haulage and it was for bringing the loaded tubs out of the mine and taking the empties back towards the coalface. As we made our way to the backs (the coalface) it grew much darker and I had to rely on my lamp. We were taken onto one of the faces to see the timbering and the coal cutter. This marked the beginning of a thirteen week course, which I passed with credit. After this training I was sent to Jubilee Colliery, West Bromwich.

I had to work on the bank for a time and I thought they had forgotten me until one day the Bank Foreman sent for me and said, "You go down the pit tomorrow." I then had to work at the pit bottom for a time and then to the endless haulage lashing tubs onto the wire rope. From there I proceeded to the backs to drive motors. At last I was working alongside the pit ponies and I took a real fancy to them.

One day the Deputy said, "I want you to drive a pony, your brother is a good driver so you should be all right after a few lessons." For a few weeks I was able to keep the same pony, until one day the stallman gave me a fresh pony - one that had not been down a mine before. He was an Arab pony and he was pretty big, but as the seam was thick we were able to drive quite big horses. I took him from the stables to the backs and placed the harness on him, and used some old shot-firing cable to attach to his head gear so that

I could drive him from the back of the tub. It was hard work for a few days but the pony settled into his job well. I then shortened the rein so that I could drive him from the front of the tub. We had to learn to change the points with our clogs. Within nine days we were bringing coal out of the backs and on to a passing loop where the tubs were sent out on the main wire. Once my foot caught in a chain and the pony dragged me away and I thought I was going to be pulled between some full and empty tubs but the motor driver heard my shouts and he stopped the pony by waving his lamp in front of the pony's face! Next day I had to carry on working with the same pony.

By now my sights were set on coalface work. I saw the Deputy and he was very good and gave me the chance. I then worked on the coalface for about two years. It was hard work but I got used to it. I then learned how the loaders felt when another empty tub appeared as soon as they had finished loading one! Some of the places were so hot and humid that I only wore shorts. I also joined the Mines Rescue Service and passed a course at the Dudley Rescue Station.

I will try to explain how we made an opening. Two roads were driven out parallel to each other. At intervals connections are driven through for access and ventilation. When the two headings have reached the boundary or fault then we started to bring the coal back. Bringing the coal down as we worked back was skilled work, and over the years was increasingly aided by machines, coal cutters, belt conveyors, and joy loaders. When I joined the 96s district there was already a coal cutter at work. One day in another part of the pit, called 9s, there was another coal cutter on heading work. It was nearly the end of a shift when someone shouted, "Jack the Overman is in the cutter." I made my way there immediately to find that Jack was in a terrible state. The machine operator had just reversed the cutter to get him out. He had lost part of his right leg and he was cut right up to his pelvis where the cutter picks had sliced into him. There was no way a tourniquet could be fitted to his leg. He was

The Mines Rescue Team outside the Rescue Station in Dudley. Ronald Adams is standing far right in the back row. Behind the team is their instructor, and to the right is the manager. Note the goggles, breathing apparatus, hand lamps, hooters for signalling to each other etc. In the foreground is the team's canary in his cage.
(Ronald Adams' collection)

still conscious and was talking to us and we got him out as quickly as we could but he died in hospital the same night.

Later I worked on a joy loader. My job was to keep the electric cable clear of the loader's tracks. We were on heading work and it did not take long to clear a heading of coal with the machine, but that meant you had to do a lot of timber and girder work to support the roof as you advanced. All the time I was learning new and vital skills, working with some of the best miners. There was a Deputies' and Firemans' class coming up so I put my name down for that, passed the course and attended First Aid classes. After a long time on the joy loaders the under manager asked me to go down the other pit on nights as a shot firer on the long wall seam.

This seam was only about 4' 6" high but as I was on the small side I could move about the face like a cat and I became a very good shot firer and first aid man. One night a man trapped his hand between the wire rope and a tree (prop). I hacked at the rope with a hammer and chisel knowing that the man was in great pain. His mate came to see what had happened, took one look and fainted. I finally cut through the steel rope and freed the man's hand. He was back at work two weeks later.

A short time after that incident I was made a full Deputy and worked days - some days in No.1 pit, some days in No.2 as I was now experienced in thick coal and thin coal seams. I was also doing quite well in the Mines Rescue Service and had become deputy leader. I was thrilled to be selected to test some new "short-time breathing apparatus" and went to the Queen Elizabeth Hospital for these tests.

One day there was a fire on No.1 Hague face at Hamstead Colliery. We had to dam the face off on the air intake side. The smoke and fumes were very thick which was very painful to your eyes. We had to use our life lines and signal to each other with hooters. After the dams were all finished pipes were put in for test purposes and we had to travel along the face every day to check the condition of the fire and the gases, setting our canary on the intake end of the coalface. My brother and I went to visit the fire with our breathing apparatus and the canary was quite well when we left. After examining the fire we returned. One of the men said he felt queer but the bird was still all right. We gave the man oxygen but as my brother looked back towards the canary the bird fell off his perch. We signalled to the rest of the team, but men who had been putting sand bags along the side of the road had all collapsed. We saved the lives of these men by putting them on the conveyor belt and getting them to the fresh air.

We were also called to a fire at Baggeridge Colliery which was a good one. We had to work four hours on and four hour off for a week, and it took two weeks in all to contain the fire. We also had many "bumps" and roof falls in Jubilee pit to deal with. One bad week six miners died in West Bromwich and an enquiry was held that concluded that machines were not safe working the thick coal and we had to go back to old methods using pit props in the openings.

One day I was working down No.1 pit as a fireman. I went into a heading where two men and a driver were at work. The heading was about nine feet high and, as I examined the roof I could see a large piece of coal which I thought looked dangerous. I decided that we would drill two holes on the face with two small charges. I examined the shot holes for breaks then began to charge the holes when an enormous bump came. My lamp was knocked from my head and you could not see a hand in front of you for dust. My legs were held fast by the material that had come down - I could not move. The stallman had jumped clear but he came back and pulled me free into a the side of the road. Immediately afterwards a girder and timber came down, and if the stallman had not stood his ground and come to my aid I would surely have been killed. I was cut and badly bruised but no bones were broken.

I was under the doctor for three weeks. I began to have pains in my neck, arms and legs. I could hardly walk about. After going to Hallam Hospital for tests I had to go for therapy for a further thirteen weeks. The doctor signed my note to say I was suffering from arthritis, but I said it was the result of my accident in the pit. They took no notice of me and sent me for a medical at Wolverhampton. The doctors advised me to leave the pit and I was awarded £18 compensation for the accident. The pit was soon to close down so I took the doctors' advice and left.

Ronald Adams today with 2 long service medals (showing front and reverse), the badge worn by the Mines Rescue Team, and a Deputy's Union badge. (Ned Williams)

Archie Williams stands by the cab of his first "Tin Lizzie" in 1926, parked by the Earl of Dudley's coal stack at the Dawley Brook Wharf in Kingswinford. Billy Tomlinson, Archie's first employee, leans against the empty sacks. Note the upturned scales on the lorry. (Archie Williams' collection)

Tales from Gornal

Archie Williams

When people talk about old Gornal they sometimes give you the impression the village was totally dominated by coal mining, and so it was to a great extent, but the place was a real hive of activity when I was a child and much of that activity was related to Gornal's other industry: sewing. Nearly every house in the village had a treadle sewing machine, and some folks had small workshops in which they had installed machines. We sewed trousers - thats all - I don't know where all the jackets and waistcoats were to be found - we just sewed trousers.

I had an aunt, who later emigrated to America, and she had a workshop at the back of her house, with four machines in, and she employed four women. All the kids became involved in this and my first experience of work was sewing the buttons on the trousers. The system worked like this: the completed trousers were taken to factors mainly living in Wellington Road, Dudley, where they were inspected and paid for. You were then supplied with another bundle of cut out trousers, linings and pockets and buttons and returned to Gornal to start all over again. These factors were Jewish, and I've heard said that Jewish folk are good at striking a bargain, but the Gornal women were their equal. and I never heard of any serious disagreements - they got on with each other very well. In fact one of them came on a trip to Gornal to see how we lived - generally they were not interested in

how we lived, or the conditions in which we worked. An old lady who lived down the Fidler's Bank embarassed him by offering him a fine piece of ham and two eggs. He declined saying he did not like ham and had never had any in his life. Later she turned to her friends saying, "How did he know he day like it effheed never 'ad anny?"

The bundles of trousers going backwards and forwards between Gornal and Dudley were carried by hand - sometimes balanced on a stick. The Gornal basket carriage was also used, even if you had to club together with others to be able to afford one. I have described these three-wheeled carriages elsewhere (see The Blackcountryman, Vol.13. No.1. Winter 1980), and they played a part in my later experiences of work. The transport problem also later played a part in my career, as you will see.

My grandfather, and his two brothers, Uncle John and Uncle Ben, were all metal workers. Uncle Ben was the most widely travelled and most experienced, particularly in the hearth furniture trade (pokers, shovels and tongs). My Grandad was a farrier and Uncle John was more of a sheet metal sort of chap. They established a small factory in Gornal - just a collection of old sheds that was a sight for sore eyes! They set up their hearths, but there were already two Smithies in the Village, Mr.Oakley and Mr.Greenaway so there really was not enough trade to go round despite the amount of horse traffic at the time. So Uncle Ben went in for making tongs. Once again the three-wheeled Gornal carriage basket came in useful. Every Saturday morning the finished tongs had to be

13

loaded in a basket and pushed all the way, mainly up hill, to Thomas Smart & Sons, Kates Hill, Dudley. The raw materials for next week's work had to brought back.

Uncle Ben had four sons and five daughters. Two of my cousins, Jack and Joe, were much the same age as me - so we were a "treble", and we worked together for Uncle Ben. We had to get some coppers somehow by honest means, and therefore we did the drilling involved in making the tongs. Two drilling machines were out in the yard - there was no room for them inside the little factory - and they were manually operated. Joe and I provided the power and Jack did the drilling. Twist drills weren't available, they were more like carpenter's bits that we worked with, and drilling really amounted to bodging a hole through! As we got to the top of each stroke the wheel we were turning lifted Joe and me off our feet.

When we had made 48 drilled discs for the tongs we were given four pence (1½p) between us. There was no wealth attached to it! And then we used to blow the money straight away on buying the Magnet and the Gem. My Aunt Alice was very rigid, I never knew her to laugh, and she recognised these comics as the work of the Devil. We would hide them in sheds at the back of the factory - but somehow she would always find them and scrap them.

We also used to fetch the breeze from furnaces near Oak Lane, where it crossed the Earl of Dudley's Railway. The coal came down by rail and was turned straight into breeze - for which there was a tremendous demand from all the local hearths. Once Uncle Ben borrowed a horse and trap for us to fetch it while I was wearing my best white suit. On the way back I sat on top of the breeze so I got a nice reception when I arrived home with a black bum. These days of working for Uncle Ben were a time when I was only six or seven years old, about 1910, but ceased when we moved up into the village and my father started a bakehouse in Louise Street. I then became my father's delivery boy and really made my acquaintance with the basket carriage, as I delivered bread all over Gornal.

By the time I left school I was expected to go into my father's business, but I detested the bakehouse. I had always disliked heat. As a lad I had to be carried out of the Zoar Chapel once or twice, simply overcome by heat. While going round delivering bread I had been gathering much good information about the work going on around Gornal. I knew the miners, and the doggies, and the chartermasters - the chaps who ran the pits and paid the Earl of Dudley a royalty for the coal they got out. There was one chap who particularly took my eye, a chap named Joe Baker. I always arranged my Saturday deliveries so that I reached his house in Red Hall Road last. He was a tremendous man physically. He hadn't enough scholarship to write his men's names down and work out their wages, but with regard to running a pit he was "it" - he was noted for it. I continually pestered him for a job.

If there was coal to get, local people always wanted to work for Joe Baker. At the time he was working Kitchen Hill Pit - one of four inter-connected pits in an area that is now part of the Pensnett Trading Estate. He always told me that my father would not let me come, but I left school one Tuesday afternoon and at a quarter past six the next morning I was standing on the pit bonk waiting to go down. I still had my schoolboy short trousers on! I went down in the cage with the doggies. Everybody called those men "doggies", said with a sneer and a feeling of reproach, because they were the gaffer's little dogs. If a bloke didn't do something right they did the gaffer's dirty work for him - and usually sacked the man.

I worked down that pit for twelve months and throughly enjoyed it. Like all lads starting on the first rung of the ladder, I was put on minding doors. I dreaded being put on the blow-george, manually turning a fan to assist ventilation: just sitting there all day long turning it - now that really did your brain good. But I was spared that and liked minding the doors.

There was quite a number of "lads" working in the four pits and they were not satisfied with the money. We were not sure how to deal with our complaints. We were supposed to be in a union but God knows where it was or who ran it - if you were running a union you kept your mouth shut about it or else you'd soon got no job - but that made our position even more difficult. One man, Arthur Wakelam, had a go at successfully running the union and had to suffer a lot of rough stuff from the bosses. He was followed by Joe Jones, but he wasn't going to suffer - he fought them up hill and down dale. He was eventually blacklisted by the Earl of Dudley. The Earl had his thumb on every pit even if he wasn't working it himself - his word was law even in the pits run by chartermasters. Joe Jones couldn't get a job anywhere. In the end he bought a second-hand bike and got a job on the Cannock Chase Coalfield, to which the Earl's influence did not extend! He had to ride over to Cannock every day from Gornal, do a day's work, ride back, and then work all night on the union stuff.

Well, we kids got together and produced a "Round Robin", a piece of paper bearing two concentric circles - our "demands" in the centre circle with our names written round the outside one, so that the bosses could not identify a ringleader. I didn't understand, but I signed with the rest. We were paid on Saturdays, when we finished at twelve. We went to a window and said our name. The money was shoved out to us in little round tin-tops with our name and number printed on. We handed our Round Robin in to the Wages Clerk.

All the following week people were talking about it. Even lads who were nearly eighteen and were hoping to become loaders or drivers had signed and we were looking forward to next Saturday. There was no word from the bosses - nothing was said. When we collected our wages the next Saturday the clerk simply said, "Doh come Monday!" That was all, there was no further explanation, they had sacked us all! I was fifteen and out of work.

I didn't tell my parents what had happened. I pinned my hopes on going to Baggeridge Pit on Monday morning. I went on the Monday and found Mr.Newey on the pit bonk. He was a marvellous man, the finest Thick Coal mining engineer who ever lived. I asked him for a job but he said, "It isn't boys I want, its men!" so there was no prospects for me there. Funnily enough that is what went wrong at Baggeridge - they just couldn't get the men. Later they mechanised the pit but even that destroyed it. They were going for the Thick Coal, the thirty foot seam but they insisted on going about it the standard way instead of following the old fashioned successful local methods. If it had been worked by our methods they would still be getting coal there today. We understood the thirty foot seam. Indeed, down at Mr. Dando's pit the seam was folded back on itself - fancy tackling a sixty foot coal face, but Gornal men could do it by the old manual methods - "Gornal born and Gornal bred,

Strong in the arm and wick in the yed."
Mr.Dandy told me how the miners had cut down saplings in Himley Wood and made ladders to get the coal. It had to be got, and miners locally always talked about "getting" coal, not mining it, and always referred to the faces as the "backs".

After my encounter with Mr.Newey I lay in the grass and cried. It looked as if I might end up in the bakehouse. Coal was going to play an important part in my future, and I would later step out the cage to see that beautiful thirty foot wall of coal again, but not for another ten years.

I went up to Gibbons Brothers and got a job in their machine shop. I worked for them from 1918 to 1926, and worked all over the place as a fitter. I installed their mechanical gas retort chargers - first perfected at Gornal Gas Works. Mr. Gibbons' son-in-law then invented a charger that could load furnaces into which items were put to be annealed, and I travelled far and wide installing these machines.

By the mid twenties I began to see an "opportunity" arising in Gornal. Jack "Dandy" Cartwright and Gibbons Brothers had been getting coal in the Cotwall End Valley - both from fairly shallow seams. In 1926 Uncle Ben followed in their footsteps in an area roughly half way between their operations, which they had, by then, abandoned. In the meantime Mr.Newey, who had refused me a job at Baggeridge, and a Mr.Allen had sunk a shaft and struck the Thirty Foot seam in the vicinity. Uncle Ben heard of their success and bought a four acre field from Mr.Whitmore of Spouthouse Farm. In the field was a shaft, seventy yards deep, which had been sunk and abandoned some thirty years earlier. It was located and deepened another fifteen yards - and there was the Thick Coal - a beautiful thirty foot wall of coal!

Whilst working out the brooch and flying reed seams Uncle Ben sank the second shaft necessary to comply with mining regulations, installed a steam boiler, winding engines and pithead gear. The roads were driven out and production began and was maintained steadily at the Ellowes Colliery until 1952. I looked around in 1926 and realised that there was a ready market for the coal from the Cotwall End Valley but the basic problem was transport. My father bought me a second-hand "Tin Lizzie" for £30, and I became a coal merchant and haulage contractor.

Unfortunately I could only afford to buy ten sacks, and therefore my one ton truck ran around only half laden at first! While saving for more coal bags I borrowed ten off Uncle Ben. He used to look as black as thunder about it, but he never said anything. When I could afford ten new bags I ordered them from Gorton's of Dudley and instead of having my initials, SAW, on them I asked for BW to be put on them. I shall never forget the look on Uncle Ben's face when I took those bags to his office. He never said anything even then, and neither did I, but I went away with the old sacks knowing it was a great day.

As my business expanded I also fetched coal from trucks brought into Dudley Station, as well as collect-

Archie Williams' coal lorry seen in a rare view of the pithead of Ben Williams' Ellowes colliery in 1936. The Cotwall End Valley is now associated with its Nature Reserve. Little physical evidence of its mining activity survives and even photographic evidence is scarce.
(Archie Williams' collection)

ing coal locally. And this is where Gornal's other industry - the sewing - comes back into the story. I realised that I had empty lorries going up to Dudley to fetch the coal so I organised the collection and delivery of the sewing. I built up quite a bit of business taking the bundles of trousers up to Dudley. It came to an end just before the War when Clifford Williams decided to establish a factory in Gornal and turn all their outworkers into factory workers.

For a while I had the only car in the village. If anybody was planning to flit I knew about it as I would get the job of shifting the furniture. If anybody was getting married they would need my car for the wedding. I even knew when the baby was due as they would tell me the date it was expected and I would anticipate getting up in the middle of the night to take them up to the maternity hospital - I was really "it". My coal wagons even had to serve as ambulances - with the tail board taken off and straw thrown on the floor we took injured miners with their feet hanging out the back to the Guest Hospital. Even Baggeridge had no ambulance until the men themselves provided one.

Eventually I ran four lorries, but it was very difficult to find good drivers during the War. We also had to cope with coal rationing and with the Miner's Allowance Coal - which is the subject of a separate story! There were also situations when it was not possible to obtain coal from the small pits and I was directed to Baggeridge Colliery. At the Land Sale Wharves of the Earl of Dudley's operation, one came across clerks who could be right "little Hitlers". They exercised great power because the regulations said we could have coal, "subject to supplies being available". At Baggeridge the clerk could make life very hard for myself and Bert Hale, the other local coal merchant. There was no love lost between us and the clerk.

I continued to be a coal merchant and general haulier until I sold out in 1960. But the business is still conducted under the same name and from the same premises. Only one lorry would now be needed for delivering coal because the domestic demand has gone. In the old times the days were never half long enough to get it all out.

The Miner's Allowance Coal

Archie Wiliams

When I began my career as a coal merchant the man who sold me the lorry was a barrister who had never practised. He lived at the top of the hill on the Sedgley - Wolverhampton Road and he became one of my first customers. When making my deliveries I always tried to make sure he was my last call. He loved to talk about Gornal, he was a good friend to me, and I knew that he would keep me canting. As things turned out he was able to give me some very useful legal advice.

Part of my work consisted of delivering the Miner's Allowance Coal. Tip top miners who worked on the coal face earned an allowance - a "coal note" that could be exchanged for a free ton of coal. This went back to the days before there were pithead baths and coal was given to these colliers so they could provide themselves with hot water for a bath in the tub in front of the fire at home. I earned four shillings for delivering the coal.

Although, in theory, only face workers were given coal notes, if a driver or loader showed enthusiasm or dedication to the task of getting the coal, he might be given the allowance, but instead of working twenty eight turns for it, he might have to work forty eight turns. The Allowance Coal was for the miner's own use. It was illegal to sell, or give away, the coal or the coal note. If the miner did not want the coal he was supposed to sell the note back to the colliery for about £4. It was very tempting to sell it to an acqaintance for £6, or to a member of the public for £8, despite the risk of prosecution. Coal merchants were often suspected of illegally buying and selling coal notes, and once an NCB inspector came to see me at a time when I had about four hundred coal notes in my house! When coal rationing was introduced miners thought they were sitting pretty if they had coal notes to sell.

My barrister friend was intrigued by all this, and on one occasion he said, "Maybe there's a flaw in the system. You mustn't sell your allowance coal, and you mustn't give it away, but they don't say anything about lending it!"

I did not give the matter any further thought at the time, as I was too busy delivering coal. One street in which I made deliveries was a terrible slum at the time, although it's changed now, and that was Bradley Street in Pensnett. On one side of the street you had to climb three steps to reach the front doors, on the other you had to descend three steps. It was the last place you would want to sell coal - and I'd got them all!

In the middle of Bradley Street was an old lady who had never registered for rationing, but somehow she always got a coal note from a collier who lived in Holly Hall. She lived alone and was never short of coal. This caused a lot of envy from those in the street with four or five children and half a ton of coal to last them three months. Sometimes this feeling boiled over, and once as I unloaded the old lady's coal a woman shouted at me, "Bloody Archie - I'll bloody shop you!"
"What do you mean?" I replied. "This is miner's allowance coal. If you want some, go and buy yourself a note. I'll risk a summons to deliver it, if you get yourself a note."
I took no more notice because people often threatened to inform but usually backed out when they had to make a signed statement to be read out in court.

When I arrived home for lunch the Misses said, "There's a lady after you; they are after your blood. You've been shopped. She has made a statement and an Inspector is coming along to see you this afternoon. He wants to interview you after he has seen the customer and the collier who parted with the note."

I thought,"That's done it." However, I got my car out and rushed over to Bradley Street. When I told the old lady what had happened I thought she was going to die, but I impressed upon her to stick to the story that she had only borrowed the note. Then I dashed up to Holly Hall to see the miner, but that was a different piece of pork. He adopted the collier's standpoint:
"It's my bloody coal. I go down the pit and earn it - I'll do as I've a bloody mind to do."
"Look," I said, "all three of us are going to face a summons if you stick to that. All you have to do is stick to my idea and insist that you only lent it to her."

"I had no faith in the collier, but luckily the Inspector went to the old lady first, then to the miner, and then he came to our house, looking all stiff and starchy, and went through my records.
"Yes," I admitted. "I've taken a load of allowance coal to that old lady this morning."
"Do you know its illegal?"
"I don't think it is in this case. It's the only coal she gets because she isn't registered for rationing."
"Well", he said...."What do you make of this - she claims she only borrowed it. I went to see the miner and he's got the same story!"
"Get on", I says.
"Well, I went back to the old lady and I said to her, 'Look here, Granny, - if you've borrowed all this coal, and you don't get any rationed coal, how are you going to pay it back?' She said:'Master, there's a good many folk who borrow a lot of money who would like the answer to that, aren't there?' Well - what could I say?"
I simply replied, "What could you say?" and I thought to myself - I'm saved!

2

MAKING IRON - WORKING WITH IRON

At one time the coal trade and the iron trade flourished alongside each other in the Black Country and were customers of each other. The geographical spread of furnaces provided a better definition of the Black Country than the presence of coal, but making iron in the area declined as the ore was exhausted. In comparatively recent times steelmaking continued to dominate the Black Country by virtue of the size of the three major works - at Spring Vale in Bilston, at the "Patent Shaft" in Wednesbury and Round Oak in Brierley Hill. The working of iron, and later steel: rolling, forging, casting, machining etc. has continued despite the fact that steelmaking has vanished. In this section we listen to two Bilston steelworkers, recorded while still producing steel, and then consider the memories of those who cast and forged the metal.

Alfred Hickman introduced steelmaking to the ironworks at Spring Vale during the 1880s. In this picture, taken in 1976, "Blitz" Barrington tests the temperature at the centre of a steel furnace. (Nick Hedges)

Bilston Steel

No book of this kind would be complete without the words and memories of the people who worked in the large steel works - indeed, they almost deserve a book to themselves. In case such a book materialises, the two accounts produced here are rather different to the others presented in this book. Instead of asking ex-steelworkers for their memories, I have used two transcripts made by Nick Hedges in 1976/77 while he took the photographs that eventually led to the publication, in 1982, of "Born to Work". These are the words of people reflecting on work while still engaged in it. Bilston Steelworks closed in 1979.

1. Syd Darby

I started work at Bilston Steelworks in 1948 - I've been here about twenty nine years. The first job I had was pig lifting. We had three old furnaces and we had twenty ton ladles that carried six tons of iron. Any iron that was left we used to run down into a pig bed, where we made pig iron. It used to be broken up when it was still hot, and when it had cooled down we had to pick it up and load it into railway trucks and it went out to different foundries. It was hard work. In those days a good worker would come and stop, but a bad 'un - he came and he looked and he went!

From there I moved onto bye-turning and then

moved on to No.2. furnace and worked there until they built this furnace in 1953. I had a job on her when her first went in. At the time we all thought we had got collar and tie jobs up here. Thats what we were told - even the Union told us the same, but we found out it was quite different. It wasn't a press button job - it was all bar, shovel and sledge.

The years went by and I worked my way up. At one time 80% of the shift managers were old furnace men. As I see it it's nice to ask a bloke to do a job if you know you can do it yourself. Now I'm a blast furnace shift manager. My responsibilities are to try and keep production the way higher management would like it. We do take that responsibilty seriously, in fact I think we put our jobs before our own families at home. We worry more here than we do at home. We get to know the men and get to know how much responsiblity we can shove on each one.

At Bilston most people have worked here a long time. Even after twenty nine years I'm only a rooky - I'm still a baby compared with some people here. I've had blokes working with me in their seventies and we had one who was eighty two! It's like being in a fishing village where everyone is a fisherman, or being in a mining community. It's the same here - it was a family concern and the works is the main topic of everybody's conversation. All your relations work here - in fact most of my relations work in the crane shop. At one time about fourteen Darbys worked there and my brother is gaffer there now. I worked there myself for a time but as my brother was the gaffer he expected more out of me than the other men.

I've been on shift work, from 2 till 10, and nights. There's a lot of time when I've been stuck here that I could have spent at home. As you get older and your children grow up you think what have I been doing all these years? I don't regret any of it really because there have been some good times, but it has changed over the years. At the moment I don't think higher management want to know about the problems we have. They say, "Let's just keep carrying on." Meanwhile the men on the furnace have lost their pride in the job. I enjoy coming to work because I've got the strength to come and I'll run any idle bugger down. I like coming so that I can run anyone down who don't

come. An Englishman's pleausure is that he can moan, we stand a lot before we turn round and grind.

Now I'm getting on, cos I've got pneumoconiosis - an industrial disease, so I ain't as fit as I used to be. Instead of my lungs being able to function properly I can only take short breaths and if I get in too much of a spin it can knock me about for half an hour. Now I've done shift work for so long I think I prefer it. I think the Monday to Friday life is a rut - doing the same thing every week and washing the car on Sunday - but of course the biggest persuader when it comes to shift work is the thirty percent extra you get for being on shifts. If they didn't pay that there would be none of us here - and we wouldn't have come in on Christmas Day for twenty five years to carry on casting.

2. Jim Dacre

I came to work in this country in 1942 - I came here in the Army, and when the War was over they put me to learning something with my brains. When I was demobbed they said I could go back to Jamaica but I still wanted to learn a trade and use my brains. British Railways trained me as a mechanic and I stayed in Paddington for six months and then I was tranferred to Foxes Lane in Wolverhampton to do general vehicle repairs. Then I left to work at Goodyears for better money, then drove a lorry, and then worked at Rubery Owen for eleven years. When they closed that plant down I came here to British Steel.

I've worked on the furnace for two years and I think we are grossly underpaid. We are being laughed at everyday. I don't know how they fix the wages on the Blast Furnace, I can't understand it. My rate is about £1.10 an hour. an ordinary labourer anywhere else gets £1.50 an hour and the women making the sandwiches in the canteen get £1.20.

We work a continental shift, Saturday and Sunday involved - Christmas - every holiday involved, and out of our group four or five work on their day off to make our money up. And on this job you sometimes

Iron continued to be produced at Spring Vale along side steel-making. The last of Hickman's furnaces were swept aside in the 1950s when the new blast furnace, Elizabeth, was built. Elizabeth was first "blown in" in 1954 and was last blown out in 1977 after producing more than five million tonnes of pig iron. Photographed in 1976, Sid Darby, known to his colleagues as "Slasher" Darby, probes the furnace just after its last re-lining.(Nick Hedges)

Jim Dacre: Bilston Steelworks 1976 .(Nick Hedges)

Working to the Buzzer

Harry Butler

I left school at the age of fourteen, during the recession of the 1930s - there was no work about. After playing around for the first two or three months I found work on a threshing machine at a farm. I had to cut the string that tied the sheaves of corn and drop the corn into the threshing box. I worked on the farm for about eighteen months, and as I was the only worker there I was doing everything, and working six days a week. I decided I would go and work in the factory, and I went to Brockhouse Castings, at Wednesfield.

At the time they were making iron and steel castings. It was 1937, and I went into a shop that was making baths, the same as the ones you can buy today. I hadn't been there many days when I started dressing the baths, picking it up as I went along, and being taught a little. Dressing was the process of cleaning up the castings and removing surplus metal. We used two great blocks of wood, like gate stumps, to put the baths on while we worked on them. One old fellow, Archie Davies, used to put the bath on its side to do the grinding and dressing. He used to get his head right inside the bath while he scrubbed the casting with an old grinding wheel. He always had his old clay pipe and his twist - and the smoke would be pouring out the bath with the clouds of dust. I don't know how he stuck it! I was bath-dressing until War broke out in 1939.

We used to make baths by hand - in a huge steel box with no top or bottom - filled up with sand over the pattern, rammed in by hand. We had to part the box, take the pattern out, close the two halves of the box, and would cast by hand. Quite a few people had their feet burnt if the metal came over the top and ran down. We put the box on a machine to vibrate it and then carried them away while still red hot.Then we had to knock the castings out. We would be covered in sand and dust. In the summer we would be stripped to the waist, as black as anything, and in a terrible state.

When the War started they turned one shop into a non-ferrous shop where they made castings for the War - for tanks etc, in brass, gun metal, and aluminium. I went into that shop to become a moulder. The conditions in there were so bad that the Factory Inspector was sent for, and he had canopies put over the furnaces to get some of the fumes away. The furnaces, about four of them, were on a stage. By turning a wheel the molten metal was tipped into a shank, and from there you used it to cast your own moulds. But the sulphur coming off the furnaces was like a thick fog.

Once again it was all work by hand. We had a bumper machine to jolt the sand down tight but everything else was a hand process. We had to put twenty boxes on the floor, on sand, put the cores in, make the tops and close them up. The fellow in charge of the furnace would shout when your metal was ready, and we would go with our shanks to have them filled with molten metal weighing about one and a quarter hundredweight. After casting the mould and they had gone cold, we had to knock them out and then start to riddle up the sand up again, water it, and prepare to start the process again. It was hard work, and I've

miss death by seconds. You can be walking around the furnace and the tuyere blow out and anything can happen. When its slagging there is too much sulphur in the slag and you cannot breathe - and when the wind is blowing from East to West its particularly bad. When we tell our wives about the work they say we should go, but the question is - where can you go? It's very difficult to find a job these days.

This furnace is very unpredictable - that's why its been given a woman's name - Elisabeth. All the Blast Furnaces are Elisabeth or Mary, I'm not joking - you never find one called Jack, or Bill, or Harry. I am the fourth man on the furnace - I'm fourth in the queue. My job is to clean the runner and make it ready for the next cast, and it is hard work. We can start to cast at any time.

We are the heart of the plant. We produce iron and gas as well. The gas from the furnace fires those boilers and it fires the soakers as well. It produces slag for your roads - it gets taken over to Tarmac. And if we didn't produce the metal the melting shop would have no metal to work with, the rolling mills would stop altogether and the chippies would all be finished. This is the only Blast Furnace in the country that is always in the black and it makes steel £10 a ton cheaper than anywhere else. We produce 240 tons of iron in one cast, then we cast again, so in one shift we make perhaps 450 tons. And there's only five of us in the team - the keeper, the first and second slagger, the first helper and me. It used to be a six-man team but they cut it to five to make more money. I would like someone to come here and tell us how to make more money!

seen people running with boxes in their hands, to get as many down as they could because we were paid on piecework - we made so much per box.

From the non-ferrous shop I went into steel castings, making anchors that weighed up to two tons. Four of us worked together in a gang, ramming the sand tight in the boxes with pneumatic hammers. We were producing too many castings for the dressers and burners to cope with, so I was moved on to the oxy-acetylene burners - I'd become a right "Jack of All Trades"! I took a liking to it. It was a bit more creative, shaping the castings with my gas jet, and cutting them. It was also lighter work but the dust blew back on me from the castings, and off the floor. I did that until 1945, when I went into the RAF for two and a half years. In January 1948 where did I go? I went back to Brockhouse Castings!

I started by cutting up scrap for them - cutting up huge pieces of scrap into small blocks that could be put back into the furnaces - dirty and dusty work again. For a time two of us were put on a project making huge drag-line buckets. I really enjoyed that - cutting them out, assembling them and cleaning them up. My mate was a welder, so I taught him about burning and he taught me about welding. It was interesting but the project fell through. I went to the dressing shop and that's where I spent the rest of my working life, a further thirty three years.

When you are retired you have plenty of time to reflect on your working life. When I look back it seems a bit like a nightmare - particularly when I think of all that dust. There was also some danger. Once there was an explosion in the shop next to where I was working. When the cold blast furnaces had finished at night they used to "drop the bottom" to extract the slag, some metal, and the white hot coke. To "drop the bottom" they would hook a chain round the prop that held the furnace doors shut, and the chain was taken up by the overhead crane which would then

Casting by pouring molten metal into sand moulds was once to be seen in foundries all over the Black Country - today you would have to search hard to find the surviving examples of casting being done in this way. (BCS collection)

drive down the shop to pull the prop out. On this occasion there was water on the floor, and when the molten discharge hit the water there was a terrific explosion. Glass and asbestos panels were blown out of the roof and all the glass panes of the crane-driver's cabin were blown out - but the driver was all right.

In the dressing shop we had a steel box, made of 1/4" steel, to put the burners away at night. The box was locked up to stop anybody on the night shift messing about with them. One night an Italian workmate was doing overtime so we put our burners away without locking the box. He must have blown some sparks across the box and someone must have left the gas turned on. There was a massive explosion which blew the lid off the box. They'd never seen him run up the shop so fast in his life.

There was plenty of work in the fifties and sixties, and the company wanted every ounce out of you that they could get. The manager called it, "Working to the buzzer." He would walk up the shop at two minutes past eight, and if someone hadn't started he'd ask, "What's up?" And he would walk around again at twenty five minutes past five to make sure that nobody had knocked off early. He wouldn't allow us time to put our burners away and gather up all the pipes. We had a lot of bother with him and his "You work to the buzzer" attitude. He even nailed a board over the clock in case anybody altered it. Little wonder that when the buzzer did go there was an almighty stampede to get out. The worst stampede was on Thursday when they gave out the clockcards showing how much you had worked in the previous week and how much you would be paid. Having collected the cards in your own time, you had to queue up to see the foreman to argue about the money.

There was one chap in our shop who was a great clown. Once he complained to the foreman that he was a shilling short in his pay packet. The foreman said, "If you're going to make that much fuss over a shilling, I'll gi' it to yo' myself." And he threw a shilling on the floor. Our chap picked it up saying, "Thanks very much, that'll save me a lot of trouble goin' through the office!" It was people like him who made life bearable. When he left you could really feel his absence the next day - there was no life in the shop. If you were arguing with the foreman he would stand about six yards away, behind the foreman, pulling faces - to make you start laughing.

I liked the people from the Black Country that came to work at Brockhouse's. They came from places like Willenhall, Bilston and Bradley, and when we recruited some Italians they had to cultivate the same sense of humour to fit in. To survive you had to be able to give, and receive, a joke. They were always playing jokes and tricks on one another, and if they could find out something you didn't like - they would give you all the more of it! I think foundry folk were like miners - they lived double lives. They could be two different people in their private and their working lives, and it was a good idea to keep your private life as private as possible, because the humour was often very personal. There was a chap called Reg Handy, he always went by the name of Andy, and he had quite a hump on his back. One day a fellow said to him, "Andy, if your head was twisted round, you'd have a smashing chest!"

Folks would get some of the shot blasting material in their hands, it was very finely cut pieces of steel, and, sometime when you weren't looking you would feel it dropped all over you and inside your clothes. You would look round but you would never see who had done it. I've even seen it done to the manager. One fellow used to put his billy can on the mould after it had been cast, the red hot metal was ideal for boiling the water in a billy can. When the manager came round he said, in his Scottish accent, "If I catch that billy can there again lad, I'll kick it off." The fellow replied, "If yo' kick that off there, it'll be the last thing yo' ever kick!" ...and he carried on putting his billy can there.

When I think about the conditions we worked in, and what we were paid, I still feel bitter about it. The way we had to work was terrible but the people were good. It wasn't just the dirt and the dust that made the environment unpleasant, it was also the noise. We endured the noise of the pneumatic hammers, the machinery, ands the shot blasts. You would have thought that everybody would have escaped to the canteen at lunchtime, but one of the memories I have of the people that I worked with is a little ring of chaps sitting in the shop round the gasjets in winter. One was a strong Conservative, the other strong Labour. Somebody would say something just to start them off - and off they would go, even though it was only three minutes into the break and they had only just got their sandwiches out. They would argue and argue. When the buzzer went one of them would look down at his sandwich to find he had only taken one bite out of it!

One chap used to sit there with his sandwiches; not like the sandwiches that everybody else had, these were that thick! And when he got down to the crust it would always find its way into somebody's tea. You would get to the bottom of your tea and find his crust. Of course, when he wasn't looking someone would try to drop a crust in his tea. By the end of the break half of us would end up with crusts in our tea. That was the sort of thing you had to put up with, but it was playing tricks like this that got us out of our rut and gave us something to laugh about while we put up with the noise and dust. At the time I had three children and was glad of the work and the security, but if I had my time over again you wouldn't see me in a steel foundry.

Smoshing Iron

Leslie Browne

Of all the trades that contributed to the name, "Black Country", I think Drop Forging came second to coal mining - it was definitely the dirtiest trade of the thirties, forties and fifties, after which things began to improve. In the old days the huge Massey hammers (4 ton and 3 ton) made large forgings for Massey Ferguson tractors. The hammer crew consisted of five men, big strong sturdy fellows who carried the forging from the hammers to the press to shear off the unwanted metal. As the forging was being made the scale would start on it as it cooled down, and, to prevent this, the hammer driver would throw in a handful of sawdust that would prevent the scale from sticking, and so make a clean forging. After every forging oil would be slopped on to the bottom

die to prevent sticking. This combination created great clouds of dirty smoke and a fine dust that would cover the crew until they looked like miners. They used sacking to cover themselves but it didn't do much good - the heat and the dirt penetrated everywhere.

Even in the die shop, where I eventually worked, we came out black because the furnaces used pulverised coal that poured through giant pipes from from the hopper to the furnaces, and these pipes used to leak the coaldust all over the factory. In broad daylight it was pitch black in the stamp shop even with the overhead lights on - and it was no better in our die shop because the big doors were always open to allow dies to be brought in and out on fork lift trucks. It was also deafeningly noisy. When I first saw Garringtons in 1948 I said to wife, "If I never get a job, I am not working in that dirty hole!" To tell the truth the job was terrifying and actually frightened the life out of me.

What led to me starting work "in that dirty hole" on 16th August 1948? And I stayed there for thirty two years, until Christmas 1980. If anybody had bet me that I would would have lasted a fortnight I wouldn't have taken them on! My life began in Dudley, but at the age of 17 I joined the Army for a trial periou of six months. I liked the army, but I didn't like marching, so in 1936 I transferred to the Royal Tank Regiment as a regular soldier. During the War I was posted to a Scottish Regiment that was going to be issued with tanks prior to going to North Africa. They were a cavalry regiment and had never seen a tank except on the newsreels so I had to teach them how to drive and maintain tanks. I went to North Africa, to Italy in 1943 and then, eventually to Austria.

I returned to Catterick to get ready for demob. I was offered a nice posting elsewhere and promotion to Sergeant Major but I had to decide between signing on for another ten years, or leaving the Army. I settled for demob. Meanwhile my parents had moved from Dudley to South Wales and I had no intention of going down there so I lived for a short time with my brother in Dudley. In March 1947 I went on holiday to Blackpool, and stayed there. I got myself a job with Vickers Armstong making aluminium pre-fabs, but their contract with the Government was running out. I went to work at Leyland Motors.

After all these twists and turns in my life it is strange to think that I still came back to the Black Country. The truth is that I met a girl from Bloxwich who had come up to Blackpool for a holiday. I had a good well paid job with a good firm at Leyland but I wrote to the girl from Bloxwich and eventually came down to see her. We decided to get married and I would move to Walsall. Leyland kept my job open for me for three months in case I found nothing in Walsall.

Mary and I decided to go job-hunting together so we caught a bus to Darlaston and we went into Rubery Owen on the Willenhall Road. They offered Mary a job on a capstan lathe atabout £5 a week, and they offered me a job as a tool-setter for about £6 a week. I decided to look further afield, and went across the road to Garringtons. They sent me down to the die-shop to see Wilf Perry. It was that dark and dirty I couldn't wait to get out into the daylight again. Huge flares lit up the stamp shop workers as each new forging was made and the hammers shook the factory to its foundations. Little multi forge machines chattered like machine guns. Mr.Perry offered me a job in which I would learn to mill the dies. I have already described my feelings about it and yet I found myself going to work there after all the opportunities I had been offered elsewhere.

When I joined Garringtons in 1948 it was a private firm but it later became part of the GKN group. At that time it was interesting to read some of the labels on the big Hydrotel milling machines such as Rolls Royce and the Ministry of Defence. These machines had been sent to Garringtons on loan for War work. We made arrester hooks that prevented aircraft overshooting the decks of carriers. We made couplings for the Indian Railways, and cutters for coal cutting machines. In small batches we made crankshafts and camshafts for submarines.

Many people who worked there lived in company houses, as they did at Rubery Owen. If you left the firm - you had to leave the house. The houses were opposite the factory and if you went in you would find everything hanging on hooks, and when the large hammers were operating everything would jump up and down - it was like living in an earthquake all the time. Even where we lived, about three miles away,

we could hear the crump, crump of the large hammers, working day and night.

Another interesting point about Garringtons was the firm's use of the canal. Our fuel, the fine coal, was brought in via the canal, and many of our products left by canal. Forgings were loaded on to the boats that were pulled by a tug, sometimes as many as six or seven being loaded at one time. Forgings for the motor trade went off to Birmingham, making the short final part of the journey by lorry. There was an another part of Garringtons on the far side of the canal where heat treatment, shot blasting and grinding were carried out. A phrase often used at Garringtons was "over the bridge" to describe the other section, and the old-timers reckoned that many dies and tools found their way into the cut, having fallen off the old Lister trucks that bumped their way over the hump-back bridge. If they had dredged the canal they could have kept the firm going for twelve months without spending a penny!

Imagine those four ton dies being carried by the Lister trucks. They were very unreliable and could easily overturn if the driver did a sudden turn. It used to take two trucks and a great deal of skill to bring those dies into the die shop. Two cranes were required to lift the die onto the twelve foot long table of my milling machine. That was another advantage of working nights - we could work the cranes ousrselves, instead of waiting for the crane driver as they did on the day shift.

In 1950, when trade was booming and every hammer and machine was working flat out day and night, a dispute arose concerning the Night Turn in the die shop. Dies had to be milled weeks in advance of their requirements and night work was very important with regard to die repair to keep jobs going. These dies would come into the die shop straight from the hammer and would be red hot. Sometimes the heat would cause the hydraulic pipes on the machine to malfunction and the die would have to be taken off the milling machine to cool down. The lads didn't like that and would do anything to get out of their turn on nights. Wilf Perry got us all together and asked for a volunteer do permanent nights in return for various financial inducements. With Mary's agreement I volunteered. The money gave us a good lifestyle, and with a new baby that was just what we needed. I bought a Triumph motorbike to travel to work and adopted a grey warehouse coat as the uniform for the job.

Soon after starting permanent nights conditions at Garringtons began to improve. The old wash-house was demolished and a new wash-house was built - with towels and special soap provided. New toilets were built and the old surgery was replaced with one of the most up-to-date medical centres in the Midlands. The die shop went through a modernisation plan that included extra windows and giant fans and heaters for the winter. Oil fed furnaces replaced those fired with the pulverised coal and the hammers were spaced out with more working space between them. The die shop was repainted, the floor was levelled and the machines were moved and repainted GKN blue. Of course, GKN money paid for this and it cost millions, but it was necessary and was very well received by all the workers whatever their job. New computerised offices were built, and a training school. Eventually the old machines were scrapped and new German machines were installed, costing a quarter of a million pounds each. Men in white coats sat at consoles pushing buttons while forgings poured out by the thousand - untouched by hand. I was coming home as clean as if I worked in an office.

We didn't regret the passing of the dark and dirty days. I had seen some terrible accidents, with arms and legs severed, and workers dying through lack of facilities. Lack of investment and bad conditions had been to blame. The lads who came to work there, unlike myself, often seemed to have known no other life. They came because their fathers had come before them. With the improvements accidents just didn't happen. Due to the dedication of its workforce Garringtons became one of the leading forgers of this century. I like to think my thirty years on the night shift played its part.

In 1974, after 26 years service, I was presented with a gold-plated wrist watch, and a tie bearing the firm's logo - a lion holding a con-rod in one paw and a crankshaft in the other. The watch is still perfect and I still wear the tie with pride. Fifty years ago we were called "iron smoshers": today they are called "forging technicians". The Drop Forge, although still used in some small firms, is gradually being replaced by multiforge machines of the future. We worked out draft angles and other complicated measurements in our heads, ground our own tools, and worked to difficult drawings that needed all one's skill. Today the machines do it for you. As surely as the chimney stacks vanish, so do the back-breaking trades of the old days.

The Lord Will Bring It Down

George Dorsett

I used to work for Hale and Hale, in Tipton, as a coremaker. I was there for eighteen years, including six away in the Navy during the War. But work became short and therefore they stopped me. (We didn't call it "being made redundant" in those days.) I thought to myself - if that's what its like working for somebody - I'll start on my own!

I don't know what made me turn to scrap. My brother-in-law was working in the scrap and before I was stopped I had worked for him now and again on a part-time basis. I asked him then if he wanted to join me in business but he said no, so I had to start on my own. I had two hundred pounds that I had saved up all those years so I bought a lorry and the business was underway.

I had to learn everything the hard way and use a lot of bluff. I didn't know anything about scrap. I couldn't tell the difference between cast iron and steel, but I'd got to make a living so I got stuck into it and bluffed my way through. By 1957 I was able to buy this yard in New Road, Willenhall.

I found a big company that was just getting going (LCP) and they asked me if I would take some engines to strip. They simply sent me a lot of engines and I had to strip them and send them back. It was hard work in those days because we had no crane and if a lorry came in with a twenty ton load of engines we had to bar them down the trailer and bar them off into the yard. After we had stripped them Neil and I had to load them back onto the lorry by pushing them up a girder.

In those days the engines had to be properly stripped. We had to take the cranks out. Nowadays foundries accept them with the cranks in but then you had to remove every bit of steel including the timing chains, the covers and the sumps. When you took the cylinder heads off you even had to knock out the pegs that were used to locate the heads. Every bit of steel had got to come off.

In the old days the small foundries would pay us more money for the old cylinder iron if we could supply it broken up into small pieces, so we used break the engines with sledge hammers - and it was hard work with those twenty eight pound sledges. I bought a crane in 1960, and Neil, who had been working for me about a year on a part-time basis, became my first full-time employee. Another major change came when we got a crane with a ball on that could be used to break up the cast iron - the ball could be dropped on the cast, breaking it all up.

I sold the engine blocks to the Dartmouth Auto in West Bromwich, or the Midland Motor Cylinder - to

George Dorset (left) puts his hand on the shoulder of Neil Buckland to congratulate him on his thirty years of work in the scrapyard. Neil joined the yard part time in 1959, and became George's first full time employee a year later when the crane was acquired. He has driven the crane ever since. (Photographed in May 1989 by the Express and Star.)

their foundries. Using the scrap cylinder iron from these blocks saved using pig iron which was about £60 a ton in those days. Scrap cost them about £13 a ton. The steel could be sold to the steel works - to Stewarts and Lloyds. They even took the sumps as light iron so there was nothing left. Ordinary cast iron went to the other small local foundries. There were plenty of them then, but nearly all of them have folded up now.

I've always had too much scrap! I buy it off firms or from travellers. I used to have a lot of cast machinery. sometimes I've had as many as eight lorries all arive in one morning with twenty tons a time - one hundred and sixty tons of scrap waiting outside my yard. Last year I took in fifteen thousand tons and sold about fourteen thousand tons out, and that's a lot of scrap from a small yard, with only one man running it.

I've had to work hard myself to build up the yard, and we've gradually bought equipment and learnt to maintain it. Sometimes I've worked all day in the yard and then driven the lorry all night. I used to go down to South Wales in the lorry to bring coke back for the foundries, park my lorry and go straight into the yard for another day's work. At one time I had three lorries but now I've only got the one skip wagon and one eightwheeler. That has to go down to Avonmouth or to Brymbo twice a day. Nowadays I employ eight men - crane drivers, lorry drivers, burners and shear operators.

In the old days it was easy to get part-timers. They would be willing to work for five bob a day. They used

to sit on the Prom in Willenhall. I used to go down in the car and say, "Anyone want a job?" I'd give them five bob each and they would work their guts out all day. In the yard the men would complain that I was "chop-choping them". They would be going away at a piece of cast with the sledge and I'd say, "Get out of the road, Gi' it 'ere and I'll break it if it kills me!" I had been in the Marines when I was in the Navy, so I used to shout, "Come on, chop - chop!"

Working in the yard has become my way of life. Blokes I've known all my life say, "Ain't it about time yo' finished?" But I've always put work first, and now I coming sixty nine and I still feel the same. The yard is open six days a week, but we also have to go in on Sundays to maintain the equipment. Of course, we have to work in all weathers. For example, I've often been soaked to the skin. And sometimes you can get injuries from working with scrap, but I've always carried on working.

I've always been very fair with my prices and I think thats why blokes keep on coming to me with scrap. A lot of the travellers come to my yard regularly, and the kids coming in today I once knew when they used to come in as children with their fathers. I don't try to do them out of anything. Whatever the scrap is worth I pay them and they know that. I've had to find new outlets for my scrap now that so many of the local foundries and steelworks have closed. Nowadays we supply British Rolling Mills at Wrexham and even export scrap via Avonmouth. My steel can still go to Duport.

I've scrapped a lot of things that I wish I'd kept. I once had a 1920s Lanchester car from Dr.Crawford. I put it in the yard and it stayed there for years until one day Neil said to me, "What are we going to do with this?" I said, "Cut it up!" - but I should have kept it. Its the same story with a very old Rolls Royce and an old Jaguar - but if I'd kept everything I would have had nowhere to put them.

I once had a future son-in-law who wanted to do some part-time work while he was in the RAF. I told him to come down to the yard at the weekend and he could work for me. So I gave him a piece of cast to break up and I gave him the twenty eight pound sledge, but he couldn't pick it up. I said, "Now look, all you've got to do is get the sledge up like this and the Lord will bring it down". So he picked it up like I had said and it went right over his head and he fell on his back.

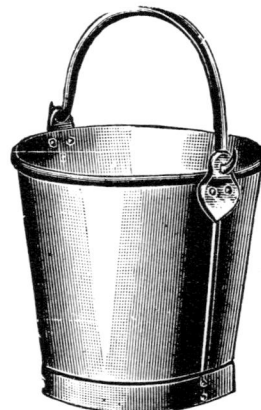

3

FIRST ENCOUNTERS WITH WORK

First encounters with work have often been childhood experiences of seeing parents or relations at work, or assisting with that work, From the accounts in this book you will see that many young people first encountered work on a part-time basis while still at school. A lifetime's work has also often started with an apprenticeship, and nowadays the Youth Training Scheme. Many apprenticeships are described throughout this book, and we catch occasional glimpses of the rituals associated with starting work and the rigours of training. Here we see one of the rituals used to celebrate the end of an apprenticeship: Tony Purchase "comes of age" as a wet cooper at Butlers Brewery, Wolverhampton, on 11th January 1961. His immersion is watched by his teacher, Mr. E.J.Lewis. Note: Although the barrels in the background have metal hoops, Tony's barrel has traditional wooden hoops - within a few years all would be swept aside by alluminium kegs, but readers can learn more about cooperage in Ralph Smiths contribution in Chapter Four.

The Straw Rope

George Edwards

My memories of work in the Black Country go back to the first decade of this century. I remember the work my father was doing and the work of uncles and cousins and my own first encounters with work.

In the early 1900s my Dad worked as an edge tool maker and his place of work was the Swindells on Northfield Road, close to Darby End. We knew it as Russells, so the Russell family must have had something to do with it. The iron arrived roughly made to shape but father had to finish the product, making sythes, sickles, hay knives, chaff knives and shovels - in fact: you name it - they made it. He was paid piecework for the number of implements he made not just for clocking on and being there.

My older cousin also worked at the Swindells, his job being to sharpen up the sythes, sickles etc. on the grinding wheels. They had huge grinding wheels driven by a gas engine, and the Swindells made their own gas on the premises, Their scythes and sickles had to be really sharp and perfect before being sent to the customer.

Have you ever seen a straw rope? Well, sometimes on a Saturday morning my Dad would take me with him to the Swindells to help him make the straw rope which was used to pack the sythes into bundles of six and be ready for delivery to the customer.

There was a bundle or bale of straw at one end of the room and I had a kind of hook and handle. My Dad would fasten the the straw onto my hook and then, as I walked slowly away while turning the handle round and round. My father fed me the straw from the bale. There you have it - that is how straw rope was made.

I was seven or eight at the time, and making straw rope was not the only thing I did in those far off days. I was friendly with the son of a furniture maker by

the name of Perry. He lived near us, on the corner of Cross Street and Halesowen Road. I spent my out-of-school hours in the furniture workshop watching Mr. Perry make sofas, chairs, tables and stools etc. I learned quite a lot about the furniture trade. We used to fetch the wood that Mr. Perry needed from a sawmill at Old Hill, together with a bag of shavings. In time I got to know what the shavings were for: the more shavings he used the less wool he used. (Wool was used in the furniture making trade in the days before foam was invented.)

We used to take the finished furniture on a hand cart or flat cart to the shops in Netherton or Old Hill for selling on to the customer. However, I eventually had leave Mr. Perry and the furniture trade because a fire destroyed his workshop. He had to move his business to a new location up Cinder Bank, which seemed a long way away in those days.

I next spent some of my time fetching the cows up to the cowshed for the local farmer at milking time.

Then I helped him make the butter, operating the churn by hand, with a handle, over and over - not round and round.

One day I heard of a baker in the area who wanted a boy to take out the bread to the customers. I can remember the baker, who was a lady, Miss Bird, saying to me, "Well, you're not very big are you?" However, I eventually got the job but I had to live in. I had to sleep on the premises because I was required to take out bread all the time, out of school hours. My wages were one shilling a week (5p), plus my keep. I always went home on Sunday afternoon and gave my mother the shilling.

I worked for Miss Bird for some considerable time, taking out bread, a basket on each arm, six loaves in each basket, until the Swindells sold the edge tool side of their business and my father had to go in search of other work. He found work in North Derbyshire, so in 1911 we went to live in a place called Seymour, near Chesterfield.

Once again I endeavoured to keep myself busy and did various spare time jobs until I was thirteen when I obtained surface work at the colliery. When I was fourteen I elected to go down the pit to become a pony driver. I always remember what a frightening experience it was to go down the pit for the first time but I soon got used to it of course. From then on that was my livelihood - down the pit.

The employees of Swindells, edge tool manufacturers of Northfield Road, Netherton, about 1910. George Edwards Snr., the father of the writer, is standing fourth from the left with his left thumb tucked in the armhole of his waistcoat. In his right hand is a hay knife, used to cut hay stacks into smaller "trusses". Uncle Sam is standing on the extreme right holding a scythe. The front row consists of young men who acted as labourers to the older men. (George Edwards' collection)

The Anvil Yard

Ted Green

Some sixty years ago I lived in a place called the Anvil Yard in the town of Cradley. As you may guess, the people who lived there made chains. The men went out into the large chain factories in Cradley Heath to work. Many of them worked at Jones and Lloyds, on the large shipping chains.

The women also made chain but did not leave the yard. Instead they worked in their own domestic chain shops. These chain shops would have two or three hearths, with a woman working at each one. The hearth burnt "gledes" - these were small pieces of coal which had already been burnt in a glede oven until the smoke had disappeared. Next to the hearth was the block. This was where the the links of chain were made. It was a large block of wood which had to be very sturdy because of the constant pounding it took. The anvil was fixed onto the block and was used to shape the links.

All the men used to work ten hour days in these chain shops, six days a week. The Anvil Yard women did outwork for a firm called Moles & Beddowes which was about a quarter of a mile away. This is how it was organised: the firm gave the iron rods to the women, the women would make the rods into chain, and then the firm used to pay them a few shillings for their labour when it bought back the chain.

I remember when the women had used all their rods they used to wrap the chain around their neck and shoulders and walk up to the firm. The gaffer would give them a few shillings, hardly anything, the women would then carry the iron rods back on their shoulders. The bundle of rods must have weighed about a hundredweight.

It was a disgrace how much they paid the women for their labour because they sold the chain for much higher prices. It was like slave labour. I always remember, some years later I was walking past Moles and Beddowes just after the War, and they had all this chain in their yard, but it had all gone rusty. Well, they couldn't sell it like that so they were putting coke all over the top of it and setting fire to it to heal it blue. I told him about it - I said, "You 'ad that med fer nothin'!" Well, he didn't like it, but it was true.

I used to feel sorry for them women, but we had a good laugh as well. I spent hours watching them make the chain, and whenever they stopped for lunch or tea, I used to try and make the chain myself. Well, I could form the links great, but I could never ever "shut" a link. And yet the women used to go, "bish - bash - bosh" and it was shut. I used to cut the lengths of iron rod for the women. When they brought the rods they were about ten feet long and I had to cut them in half. To do this you had to "bally" the rod on your finger. When balanced you marked it and then you could cut it. It had got to be dead centre. If you didn't get it dead centre they would give you a right "pailin", because if you had cut them short you got extra scrap, and the women wouldn't get paid for scrap.

I remember the women with babies used to put the babies by the hearth, wrap them up and stick their dummies in. The women would be singing away, making the chain, and I have sat with them for many many hours. Mind you, some of the women were corkers. I always remember one day we had a visitor. He was a new Baptist minister and he wanted to see how these poor unfortunate people lived. Well, I was with my mate and we decided we ought to show this minister how they made chain. So we took him to see Maria. She was going away at it and singing.

"Won yo' wont?" she said. I told her we had brought a friend who wanted to see how she made the chain,

and I told her he was the new minister. She didn't seem to mind, so I told him to come round and stand at the front. Maria was there and she pulled out one of the links from the fire. It was white hot and ready for welding. She put her hand in the bosh and scooped some water out and threw it on the bikkon. Well, I knew what would happen next and got down out of the way. As she brought the hammer down on the hot iron it went off like a gun. It frightened the minister to death and he was off. You see, the women didn't like to be watched, and this was one of their dodges to clear folk off.

As I've said, the women worked very hard and long, and there was a real skill needed to make the chain. I could never master it. I don't think anybody who didn't work in or around chainmaking could ever really appreciate how bad it was. Although I look back and have a lot of fond memories, I'm glad those working conditions have gone.

Note: Ted Green was born 13th June 1911, and in later life always referred to himself as a "true Anvil Yarder". It was one of those communities within the larger community that was such a feature of the Black Country. Ted loved the Black Country and the people of the Anvil Yard in particular, and he lived there until it was pulled down. As he says here, he was not able to make chain, and so he worked in local brickyards and the pits. His concern for the exploitation of the women in the Yard later encouraged him to join the struggle to improve the lives of working people, and he was also able to pass on vivid memories of that struggle. He died on 24th March 1989, having recorded his memories for April Garratt, who made this transcript.

The Anvil Yard, Cradley, around the turn of the century. Photographers did attempt to record the squalor of the chain makers surroundings and their primitive working conditions.(Birmingham Public Libraries)

The Stone Breaker

Cecil Westwood

In the early years of this century the quarries at Rowley employed men as "Stone Breakers". Even in earlier days there were mechanical crushers which could supply granite in a variety of forms ranging from huge chunks to small chippings or even dust. Even so, the human stone breaker was needed to produce stones about the size of an orange, although irregular in shape. I knew one man in particular to whom, as a lad, I walked over the banks before going to school to take his breakfast.

With a small roundish hammer, on a long slender shaft - the length of each shaft varying to suit the height of the man using it -he stood over his work making an up and down movement with his body as if it was on a hinge. This movement was repeated hundreds, perhaps thousands, of times in a day. He usually held the large piece of stone down with his foot while his downward movement with the hammer was applied to it. Thus was the large piece of stone reduced to pieces of the correct size. It was a menial and back-breaking task, but it required a reasonable skill to accurately produce stone the right size.

He had little time to stand and stare, except maybe for a moment to lift his gauze-fronted goggles up onto his forehead, perhaps to light his pipe or sit down for a moment. Sitting was difficult as he was perched on a heap of stone that was gradually getting higher and higher. The heap of stone was known as "The Ruck", and it was situated on the side of slightly rising ground. Stone to be broken was tipped onto it from trucks known as "Tubs". Although the heap of stone gradually increased in height, the company knew exactly how many tubs the workmen had broken in one week and the stone breakers were paid accordingly. Hard earned wages indeed!

Upon returning home each evening the stone breaker that I knew well became a bookman - reading and studying works of Theology together with the best of general literature he could afford to acquire. On Sundays he was still figuratively a stone breaker. As a Methodist Lay Preacher his hammer was the Gospel which he applied to those who had stony hearts!

I knew this man very well; he was my father.

Stone Quarry workers at Rowley Regis Granite Quarries in the 1920's. The stone from this quarry provided road foundations and chippings were supplied for surfacing. (BCS Collection)

First Impressions at Baldwins

Archie Clarke

In 1932, at the age of fourteen, I started work at Baldwin's Steel Works, Swindon, known locally as "Swin Forge". On the first morning I set out at 6.15.am. as I had more than a mile to walk and the starting time was 7.30.am. I wore blue bib and braces overall, and carried my sandwiches in a small wicker basket and a bottle of tea in my pocket.

Arriving at Swindon I passed through some large cast iron gates and, as instructed, waited for my Uncle who had obtained the job for me. He met me and led the way up some concrete steps and into the mills. This was another world, and one that I found exciting and frightening. The noise was so loud only a shout could be heard and the air was filled with the smell of smoke, steam, and hot steel. In spite of large gaps in the corrugated iron walls and the wide vent which ran the whole length of the high roof it was like entering an oven.

Some distance away was the line of six sets of huge steel rolls, each backed by two furnaces. Bright red steel bars were fed into the rolls, then lifted back over the top roll to be fed through again. The process was repeated until the bars were elongated into dull red sheets. Small groups of men huddled round each pair of rolls, using steel tongs of varying lengths like extensions of their arms. they were dressed in collarless shirts, trousers, and clogs, and each man had a towel wrapped round his neck.

It was an incredible scene, flames leapt from furnaces as the doors were opened, and red hot steel was being moved everywhere. Steam driven presses and shears were in operation, adding to the general air of frenzied activity. Although I did not know it then, some time later I was to spend some years working there in the mills.

We passed the huge steam engine which drove the rolls, set in a pit below floor level. The gigantic piston travelled to and fro, and the large fly wheel rotated quickly. This engine worked twenty four hours a day and for five and a half days a week. It was stopped for only fifteen minutes when the shifts changed, three times a day.

Leaving the mills we reached the centre of the works where a line of men filed past a large clock, inserted a card, and pressed a lever to register the time: the day workers were clocking in. These men were a small minority of the employees. Most men were simply paid for the tonnage of steel they processed. Watching the clocking operation was a tall gaunt man, wearing polished boots, a dark blue suit with a gold watch chain looped over his waistcoat. He was the timekeeper, disguised as an undertaker or civil servant. He was not very civil to me when I used the clock for the first time.
"Hey Laddie," he said, "That's a lever not a punch ball - just press it gently in future!"

He led me through a shearing shop and then a pickling shop. Men wearing rubber boots and aprons, with cloths covering their mouths and noses, worked over lead-lined troughs of acid. Although there was ducting over the troughs to carry away the fumes, the air here was acrid and stung the nose and eyes.

It was pleasant to emerge into the open air at the rear of the works, where large wooden packing cases were stacked high in piles. New ones were stored under the corrugated iron roof of a lean-to shelter which ran the whole length of the building. In the centre of the shelter was a wooden bench where a man and a boy were hammering nails into a packing case which lay on the bench. Work stopped, and my Uncle made the introductions. "This is your boss: Mr.Smith. Just do whatever he tells you," said my Uncle turning to the slightly built man who wore glasses, a cap that looked too big for him, and a worried look. "This is my nephew, Archie Clarke, if he doesn't do what you tell him, kick his arse!"

With that wonderful exit line he walked away. For a pillar of the Methodist church, I thought he excelled himself. So I started my working life with what might be called a little instruction. For the next eight or nine months I worked with Bert Smith and two other boys repairing old cases, and nailing on strips of steel to reinforce new ones. Every day we delivered a number to the packing shop, using a large hand cart.

Working hours were from 7.00.am. until 5.30.pm., Monday to Friday, 7.00.am. to 12.00 on Saturday morning. There were two meal breaks, one at 8.30.am. to 9.00.am. and one at 12.30.pm. to 1.30.pm. At these times a number of men would come to the cases shed to eat their meals. Bacon and eggs would be cooked on a shovel, over a steel box full of red hot coals shovelled from the tin house furnace. Toast was made heating a flat piece of steel until red hot, held in short tongs it was passed over the bread as a mobile grill. This method was also used to heat bacon which had been cooked at home.

My next job was in the Tin house, where I worked in the "trough" with three other boys, cleaning the oil from sheets that had been plated with tin. The sheets were first pickled in acid, submerged in two vats of molten tin, and then given a final dip in hot oil. From the rack on the platform where these operations took place, two boys carried each sheet to a shallow wooden container standing on legs two feet high. All the edges of this large open box were covered by sheep skins to prevent the sheets from being scratched. This was the "trough" - aptly named as it was kept half full of "Sharps", an animal food slightly coarser than flour, fed mainly to pigs. Each hot sheet was lowered into the trough and sharps rubbed over its surface by sheepskins which the boys wore on each hand. A second pair of lads then hauled the sheet on to a padded table and polished it with pads of soft duster material.

The work caused clouds of fine dust which turned all clothing white. Brushing and patting removed the surface dust but helped the rest to become ingrained. Boys who worked at the trough were permanently dressed in off white clothing, like millers.

Between batches or "heats" of work we would spend a few minutes outside on the wharf of the canal which ran down the whole length of the works. This was a busy area as all steel and coal was delivered by boat and unloaded by hand. Most of the steel produced left by the same route but cranes were used to load outgoing traffic. Coal and slack were unloaded by a team of men using large shovels known as "banjoes", into huge wheelbarrows which held approximately two hundredweights. The steel bars, twelve to fifteen feet long were unloaded near the mills. Three men carried each bar out of the boat, lifting, walking, and stacking them on the bank in perfect unison.

During my first year at work there were two serious accidents, and I knew both victims personally. The first was in the shearing shop, and some time after the accident I went there with a workmate. The shears were roped off, awaiting a visit by the factories inspector, but on the ledge behind the blades were the top joints of three of the shearer's fingers, lying where they had been sliced off. The second accident occurred in the tin house. To lift the sheets from one vat of molten tin to the other, one man stood with one foot placed in the small space between the two vats. Harry Massey, one of the team we worked with, stood in this position about eight times every day, for the ten minutes it took to transfer the sheets. On this occasion his foot slipped into the molten metal. Harry was off work for months, was partially crippled, and was never able to resume his job in the tin house.

These were the kinds of first impressions I received at Baldwins, before going on to work in the mills. Even then the works was very out of date, and I realise now that methods and machinery had hardly altered since the turn of the century - but the team work required in those circumstances created a wonderful spirit amongst the workforce.

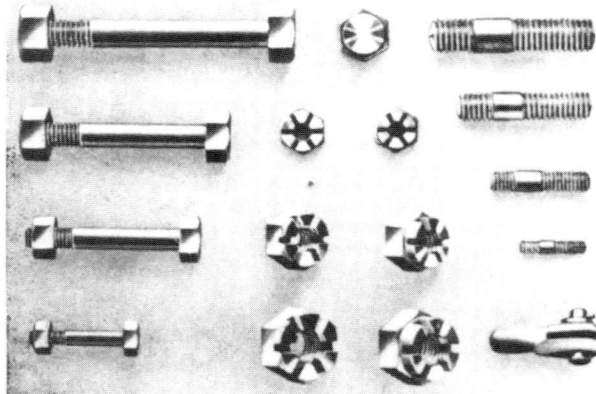

Starting Work at Rubery Owen

Malcolm Timmins

It was in 1935, at the age of fourteen, that I started work at Rubery Owen, Darlaston. I had realised before leaving school that factory work wouldn't be pleasant. However, nothing that I had visualised prepared me for the reality. The noise, stench and filth were all far worse than I had expected but the biggest shock of all was the working hours - they seemed interminable. From 7.30.am. to 6.00.pm. Monday to Friday and 7.30.am. to 12.30.pm. on Saturday constituted the normal working week.

The usual starting wage was 10/- (50p) a week. Out of this Dad gave me 1/- (5p) as my pocket money, which in those days bought me sweets, ice-cream and at least one visit to the pictures. At the age of fifteen wages rose automatically to 12/6 (62½p), and with an increase in pocket money to half a crown (12½p) I began to experience real wealth. Sadly being fifteen carried a penalty - I was now expected to work over-time if required. Many of the adults, with whom we youths worked, routinely stayed until eight or nine o'clock, whether they had any work to do or not, and we lads had to stay on with them. On Saturday, unless they happened to be football fans and their team was at home, four or five o'clock was the norm for many men. Of course, there was as much as five bob (25p) overtime pay, but this was poor compensation for the loss of treasured leisure hours.

In factories in those days school leavers didn't go to fill any specific job: you either went "in the office" or "in the works". The normal procedure in the works was for the foreman to take the newcomer round the various charge-hands until one was found who was willing to take the risk of setting the lad on. Anyone who wore glasses - which I did - was usually very difficult to place. There was a widespread feeling among working class men of those days that anyone who admitted that he needed glasses was either simple minded or, at best, a cissy.

I always remember being taken to one charge-hand who, squinting at me with screwed up eyes, said emphatically, "I can't have him, Fred. He'd be a danger to himself and everybody else, wearing glasses!" I later discovered that this man was unable to see the check number on his time card, which was a quarter of an inch high. He had to ask a confidant to find it for him so that he could "ring in". He couldn't read or write either, but in those days it didn't matter too much.

Eventually I was taken on by the bloke in charge of making Citreon chassis frames - yes we used to make components for Continental car firms in the old days. After all, Mr.E.Owen virtually invented the motor chassis frame.

Whereas, in more recent times there are often as many managers, supervisors, and assorted office staff, as there are production workers, in my early days at work the whole department was run by one foreman and a young girl to help him with the office work. Fred was a foreman in the old tradition. He had a well worn shiny blue serge suit, a gold (?) "Albert" across his ample belly, and the obligatory cloth cap. If a problem arose it was quite normal for Fred to take off his jacket and sort things out in person. No foreman of that time would dream of expecting his workmen to do anything that he wasn't capable of doing himself.

Paraffin was everywhere. It was used as a general cleaning agent. Products were washed down with it in preparation for painting, and everyone used it to wash the dirt from their hands. As can well be appreciated, skin complaints were common but this was not the most serious consequence of its use. the clothes of the men who wiped down work prior to its being painted were always saturated with paraffin, and on at least one occasion a man lighting his pipe from a fire-bucket caught fire and burnt to death. There were several fatal accidents, including one where a man who lost his footing fell into a vat of enamel and drowned.

Without doubt the happiest day of the week was Friday - pay day. There were no sealed pay envelopes then. Wages were in metal cups which came from the Wages Office secured in wooden trays. The cups were in holes numbered to correspond with the employee's check number.

An essential part of the pay day routine was the exchange of wipers. Each week all the employees were issued with a coarse-woven cloth, about one foot square, with which to wipe his hands. By Friday these wipers were fithy and contained quite a generous amount of oil. The firm that supplied them took them back, cleaned them, and in the process recovered a worth-while quantity of oil. The wipers were then re-issued to collect another week's supply of recoverable oil.

Married Women Need Not Apply

Dot Davies

I grew up in Wolverhampton and my father was an engineer and millwright. In the mid twenties he was installing machinery in a brand new factory being built for Courtauld's, in Whitmore Reans. As the work finished he was asked to stay on and become a works fitter. At the same time I was reaching school-leaving age and so my father put my name down for a job there. There was not much work about at the time and so anybody who got a job was lucky. I was one of the lucky ones - I was given a job in the Reeling Department and started the same week as the factory opened - in 1926.

Courtaulds Ltd. were a Coventry based company and at first ten girls from Coventry were sent over to teach us the job. When we were trained they went home and we trained the next girls, and so on. The first threads of viscose rayon were spun in the September of 1926 and production of artificial silk was underway. In coming to Wolverhampton Courtaulds had said they were attracted by "a supply of the right sort of female labour". By that they meant we had to be young and single. It was certainly a new and spotlessly clean environment in which to work- the toilets were wonderful but you couldn't spend too long in them!

I earned 9/lld (just under 50p) for my first fifty six hour week, which included a Saturday morning. It was a 7.30. - 5.30. day and occasionally we could earn overtime by starting at 6.30.am. Every six months I received a two shilling a week rise and I worked there for ten years until I was twentyfour. By then my wage was 32/lld a week full rate, or I could earn 36/lld (£1.85.) with overtime. I was lucky to have a job and there were good facilities - like lunch in a canteen and free milk during the "tea" break during the morning but the kind of labour they wanted was "slave labour"!

I had to reel the silk onto skeins. It arrived in its raw form in hanks and I put it onto the collapsable arms of my machine. It was work where you used your fingers all the time, as I pulled a strand out and tied it on with a weaver's knot. The silk went from us to various other departments such as the sorting and bleaching departments until it ended up in a very shiny state. If you had the slightest bit of roughness on your fingernail it would split a thread on the skein and it would have to be scrapped - and you would get into trouble! The skeins were inspected in the Sorting Department and if they weren't perfect the foremistress would come along and shout at you. When I finished I was running about twenty machines and teaching about six newcomers as I went along. I was really experienced.

Our machines were in rows and we sat opposite one another and were able to shout to each other. We had a lot of fun and I enjoyed working there because of the way we could chatter:
"What did you do last night, Dot?"
"Oh I went out with Clark, you know - Clark Gable!"
We loved making up things we were supposed to have done the night before and we could sing as we worked. We could make as much noise as we liked as long as

we got the work done. The one thing that was absolutely forbidden was getting married. My sister also worked in the same department but she had to leave after six years when she married.

I had been engaged for two years and wanted to get married myself but I would not get married until we had saved up enough money to buy furniture and start a home. I took a great risk and we had a secret wedding. We told nobody at all, except the two friends who were our witnesses at the Registry Office. When I went to work I carried my wedding ring in my bra and desperately hoped not to get the sack before we had furnished our home.

On one occasion, Mr.Nightingale, one of the bosses, came across to the room where we worked and went up to a girl about twenty yards away from me. Afterwards I learnt that he had said, "Good afternoon Mrs...." She looked at him and he said, "You are Mrs..... aren't you?"
"Yes."
"Then get your coat and get out!"

From then on I always felt worried about my secret. Everytime someone came near me I expected to be sacked and it was affecting my nerves. There didn't seem much hope of becoming a foremistress because the boss had said, "We'll never let you off the machines - you're too good a worker and nobody can run as many machines as you." In the end I was so worried that I left - but we had managed to furnish our house from top to bottom for eighty one pounds and threepence.

The Courtaulds factory under construction - Dot's father worked on the installation of the machinery and put her name down for a job at the factory. Cyril Lord (on page 60) describes his experience of building the factory including the base of the giant stack on the right. Charles Dickinson (on page 66) describes erecting the kind of steelwork shown and refers to the kind of derrick that can be seen in the foreground. (Photo: Wolverhampton Public Libraries)

4
MADE IN THE BLACK COUNTRY

As the reader will see from the following accounts, the Black Country was remarkable for the variety of its products, and the materials from which they were made. However, our reputation and image depends to a large degree on "metal bashing". Having made iron, and later steel, our local industries were based on our abilities to forge it, cast it, roll it, machine it etc. Let us begin a chapter on making things by illustrating the manufacture of wrought iron. Pig iron arrived from the ironworks and went into the puddling furnaces, to be smelted then shingled and forged. In this picture the hot ball of iron has been raced to the steam hammer from the furnace on the two wheel trolley held by the man on the right. The shingler is grasping the ball with his tongs and placing it beneath the hammer. The shingler and the hammer driver, seen in the sheltered shadows on the far left, will then work in partnership to hammer the iron into shape. This picture was taken at the turn of the century in the works of John Lysaught Ltd., Wolverhampton. This company produced iron in the form of sheets, that could be galvanised, and in the form of bars and billets, in a large works at Horseley Fields. Huge castings were produced in their foundry, including fly-wheels of twentyeight feet diameter, weighing over sixty tons. These castings were then machined in huge lathes. Bars and sheets could be produced on a similar massive scale. In turn, these products became the raw material from which many local products were made. (Author's collection)

*This female nailer from Cradley was featured on a John Price postcard, printed in Bilston. Note the short dumpy hammer used by nailors and the nail rods standing by the window.*Dave Whyley's collection)

FemaleLabour at Cradley. 679

Makin' Nails

Emma Whyley

My father was named Samuel Tromans, he was a nail maker, you know - he made nails. But, you see, it wasn't ordinary nails he used to make - it was ones with brass tops on for horses' saddlery.

He worked for a firm at Walsall - Packers at Walsall, I think. He used to send his work to them every Friday night from Blackheath Station. We had to bag it and put the tally on, and it used to go by rail to Walsall. Then they used to send his money every month.

At first he worked with his father in Darby Street, Blackheath - you know, the second house from the Chapel, but when his father died he worked in the nail shop behind our house in Long Lane, Blackheath - Worcestershire that was.

We had a shop with three hearths in, and it was a coal place as well. My two oldest sisters made nails with him, our Annie and Esther. I tried, he put me on, but I couldn't do it. There used to be an old cripple as used to come and sit on the side of the hearth and sometimes blow the bellows. Jake it was, he lived in New England.

Every now and again, you know while I was working, my father would drop a rod of iron across my shoulders and he would shout out:
"Bend thee back - Bend thee back oosn't."
and I can see Jake now you know. He said:
"Sam, Sam. it's no use thee a botherin' with her yer know, 'cause er'l never make nails. Her ay got it in her."
So after a while I was put in service for Mucklows.

To make the nails we had a thin rod of iron and we used to heat it up with gleads. Then you got it out, bent it, put the point on, and hammered the top and then put the brass part on. I can't quite remember how the brass part was put on, whether we knocked it on or not. My father just worked an 'and hammer, because the nails were only small, and a pair of bellies (bellows) to blow the fire.

When I was small, you know - a little girl, I didn't blow the bellows for him, but I used to carry the iron from the bottom of Rowley, up to the top of Long Lane and, being thin, it used to be in a ring. Ar, I used to have to go and fetch the iron for him.

When Annie and Nancy got married there was only father as worked in the shop. I can't remember how much he got paid for those nails, but it wouldn't be much. My mother nailed you know. Her used to do a bit at night, and there used to be a shop on the corner of New England, and he used to buy these nails off her, but it was very rare we had the money - we had something out of the shop instead.

Well, her's gone many a time and got we a pair of shoes like that. There were nine in the family for my mother to look after and there were four of we little ones; and she used to put the maiding tub by the back door and stand we in the tub to have a wash. There used to be wooden shutters on the nail shops in them days, and her used to keep the shutters open in the nail shop as she could see we, and she would keep shouting to we - we should be a-washing in the maiding tub while her was a-nailing.

Note: Emma Whyley, nee Tromans, was born on 17th November 1893 and died in 1985. David Whyley, her grandson, made the recording and this transcript based upon it. It was recorded 22nd November 1979.

Best, Special and Beezer

Dennis Barnsley

I was seventeen when I started making chain - that would be in 1945. Well, as it happened my father said, "Yo' am comin' with me to mek chain". My Dad had made chain all of his life, and mother made it, and my grandfather and my grandmother made it - it was all in the family, so that's how I came to make it.

My Dad was working at Richard Sykes & Sons, Cradley Heath, at the time. You know Sykes was a separate company but they worked under Hingley's. So I started at Richard Sykes with my father.

When I first started we had to set the block up. I had got to make 5/8" chain. My father said, "Nobody else is going ter learn yo'. I'm going ter learn yo'." Sykes had got a training officer who was gettin' on, and that's what they got him to do - train folks, but my father said he wouldn't let anyone else learn his son.

Well to set up the block - it took two days to get it right. This was a big shop - I should say about forty hearths. Then my Dad showed me how to heat up bars, how to bend, how to get the proper heat to scarf out, how to get the welding heat, and how to "tommy". You had to be careful not to overheat it or, if you hit it, it would just scatter the iron if it was too hot. It took me about a month to learn how, and then I was set on properly, but all the chain that I made in that month was not wasted, it was sold.

My father said, "I'll see yer right for all that chain as you've med. When you go piece work on yer own, you'll only get paid for what you've med from a place on the chain marked by a piece of wire that the foreman will put in." Well, when my month was up and the foreman put the wire in to start me on piecework, my father got the wire out of the chain and he put it back about four or five hundredweight to give me a good start. You could say I had five day's start!

When I was making 5/8" piecework I could expect to make 184 links in six hours - that was about a hundredweight or so a day. We could start at five o'clock in the morning, but I'd go in at six and knock off about half past twelve. Dad used to knock off earlier because he was faster than me, then he would go over Llewellyns for a pint, and he would say, "Come on over for a pint lad, I'll treat yer." Of course, we always had the beer on the strap and paid on Saturday when we got our wages. We got paid on Saturday breakfast. After that they day get much work out of 'em 'cause they was over in the pub. They dare not pay them on a Friday 'cause then they wouldn't come in on a Saturday.

When I first started I got paid about £9 a week for one hundredweight a day for six days which was a good wage. We had a set price book so that we could check up what we had coming. There were three types of chain - "Best", "Special", and "Beezer", and "Beezer" was the one you got extra for, but I'll tell you, that had to be "bang on", that had.

My Dad made all my tools to start with. I helped him knock the "point" in while he showed me how to do it. He made all of my tongs. At that time there were a few people there who could knock up a pair of tongs in twenty minutes, forge the ends, and weld the reins on and rivet them up, and all they would ask

Dennis Barnsley tommying a link on the oliver in the Mushroom Green Chainshop in the early eighties. (Photo: David Whyley)

for them was half a crown. It would save you that in time, 'cause if you weren't used to making tongs it might take you an hour.

I went to the gaffer twice and said, "I need a new hammer."

"I'll tell you where to go," he said, "round the corner goo to Richard Greens." They used to make the hammers there, and they would ask you whether you wanted a 2lb. or 2 1/4lb. one and you would tell them. A bloke would weigh out the steel and mek it into shape and you had to go and fetch it when it was finished. The you had to get a hammer stale off the foreman and put it in yourself.

I'll tell you about the clothes we wore. It was a "ganzey" - a hand-made vest. I would say to Mom, "The ganzey is all in holes." and she would go to Cradley Heath Market and get some flannel. And then she would sew it all up and put a big patch on the front made from "ducking" - to stop the sparks burning you. The best trousers you could get were army trousers. They were thick and they used to last, but once you had worn them for say a month they had to be put on the line everyday to dry, because they were always soaked in sweat. After a month you could stand them up like a board - stiff with salt! Army & Navy Stores boots were good - they would last even if you trod on a red hot coke. Well, this is how we got our aprons - this bloke who collected the union every Monday, he knew somebody on the railway who had some old tarpaulins, and he would cut

Sparks fly as Dennis Barnsley shuts a link on the oliver at the Mushroom Green Chainshop in the early eighties. (Photo: David Whyley)

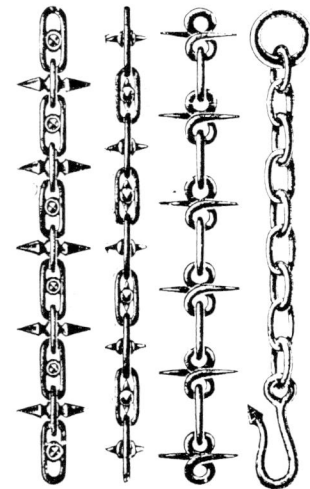

them up into squares and charge 1/- for an apron. They were good.

Burns were bad, particularly burns in the eyes. You were sweating and when a spark came towards you, you always seemed to catch it between your eyelids, and they would be stuck together. All you had to do was scrape the spark off with your fingernail and carry on. On the back of your hands you had red hot scale going on everyday. Of course you could not loose the link 'cause you were hitting it with one hand and holding it with the other. You just had to suffer it. If a spark went down your boot, the only thing you could do was get your foot and put the whole lot in the cold water bosh to cool, saying, "Oh, that's bloody lovely, that is!" Then you would carry on - you hadn't got time to undo your laces!

I took a bottle of tea and a slice of bacon, and two rounds of bread, with me to work. You drank part of the tea and then kept on filling it up with water. It was diluted that much in the process of drinking at least ten to eleven pints of water a day to replace the sweat as you were working. You could stop to eat - we would get the scovern, get it hot, dip it in the water to clean it, then put the bacon on and cook it over the fire, and then put it on the bread: it was lovely. That was your breakfast - then it was back to work.

I used to like making 7/8" stud chain best. I did make 1" for a while on my own, but I should have had a striker. My Dad said, "Doh mek it on yer own, lad, it'll kill yer." I did make it - but not for long, it was very hard work. The end links were thicker iron and you needed a striker to "shut" them, so you asked a mate, and then used a large hearth when the others had gone home. We helped one another out.

We could see the end of the trade coming. All the talk in them days was of electric welded chain, but we used to say to ourselves, "It'll never come, 'cause they cor weld wrought iron - and wrought iron is the best." But they made electric welded chain from steel: it wasn't so good of course, but it took over our job. People kept on leaving and I was put on short time. When I left there were only three chainmakers in our shop: me, Jack Shaw, and Freddy Fellows. I left the trade in 1959 and got a job up Austin's in the forge. However, I still make chain at Mushroom Green Chain Making Museum, to demonstrate the old trade.

Not anybody can make chain, you know. There's a skill in it, and you've got to be born into it. It's a skill as the ordinary working chap cor do. It's just got to be bred in a chap, like in my family.

A Life on the Block

Lucy Woodhall

I was born Lucy Swingler in Clyde Street, Old Hill, in November 1899. My mother was a nailmaker, but I never saw her actually making nails. During my time at school the class I enjoyed most was needlework and my teacher said that I would do well in the dressmaking trade. I remember saying to her, "No Miss, I am going into the chain trade."

I left school on my thirteenth birthday, a Friday, and started work as apprentice chainmaker the following Monday at Hortons in Old Hill, November 1912. Before I could start my two year apprenticeship I had to pass a medical examination. This was carried out by a visiting doctor and took place in the boss's kitchen. I passed this with flying colours.

My training started by having to pump hand bellows all day to provide the air-blast to keep the hearth fires going for the chainmakers in my shop. Occasionally, as a relief from this, I was allowed to go "on the block" - an iron block into which was wedged the various tools used for making chain. I could practice "turning a link" - bending the end of a hot iron rod into a "U" shape, the first stage of making a link, and later "shutting a link" - the art of fire-welding together of the two open ends to form a flat-sided oval link. I also had to sweep up the chainshop and, on Saturdays, clean out the works lavatories. When I first started the work the hours were seven in the morning till seven at night, Monday to Friday, and seven till two on Saturday. For this my wages were were four shillings a week. (20p) The works always looked clean and tidy because the last thing we did before finishing on Saturday was to sweep up.

After I had been there for six months my wage was increased to five shillings and six pence a week. (32½p) After twelve months I was put on to "stint" work. A stint is a specified amount of work to be carried out. If this was completed before the normal finishing time you had the choice of going home early or staying on and carrying on working. All the extra chain made in that time was weighed on Saturday and you were paid the piecework rate for it. If I had a good week the extra piecework pay was as much as two shillings and six pence (12½p), which was a lot of money in those days.

Not long after I had completed my apprenticeship I moved to my next job, at William Stevens, in Brook Lane, Old Hill, known locally as Steven Cooks. By this time the Great War had broken out, and I was on piecework making military harness and other chains that were needed for the large number of horses used in that war. At the age of nineteen I left William Stevens and moved to Hollingsworths, in Meredith Street, Cradley Heath. There I learnt how to "bolt" swivels - the very skilled job of making swivels used on harness work allowing greater movement of the chain. I worked with four other women making "country work" - cow, bull, and calf ties and traces etc. My working hours by this time had been reduced a little to 7 till 5 on weekdays and 7 till 12 on Saturdays. my wages had increased to thirty shillings (£1.50) a week.

After about four years I moved to Harry Stevens of Oak Street, Old Hill, where I settled down and stopped for about thirty five years. When Harry died

Lucy Woodhall shutting a link. (Photo Ron Moss)

his son, Mark Stevens, took over the works. I was on day work, and the working hours were 7 till 5 weekdays, and Saturday mornings. These times were later altered to 8 till 1 and 2 till 5 weekdays, 8 till 1 Saturdays. A little later we finished at one o'clock on Mondays.

After a while I was trusted with the keys to the works, and I was expected to turn my hand to anything - such as loading and unloading the wagons, and attending to the various "outworkers" that lived close by the works. Outworkers were men and women that collected iron rod from Mark Stevens to make chain to order in their brewhouse chain shops behind their homes, and then brought the finished product back to the works where they were paid for their labours.

By the 1950s I was the only woman chainmaker in the works, and I watched the number of men dwindle from four to three, then two. In 1958 Mark Stevens died, and this was a very sad day for me. The works closed and the trade was taken over by Samuel Woodhouse & Sons, Corngreaves Road, Cradley Heath. I was asked to carry on making chain for them at their works, and found myself in a small chainshop with three men and two women. I watched these leave one after another until I was left working in the shop all alone. I carried on making chain until Christmas 1973, when the pain from arthritis in my leg forced me to retire at the age of seventy three. I had been making chain for sixty years and one month.

Note: Lucy Woodhall was probably the last woman chainmaker to make chain by hand in Great Britain. She died in Dudley Guest Hospital on 11th October 1979.

Over a period of about ten years she made tape recordings for Ron Moss and passed information on to him from which he has prepared this autobiographical account. Ron Moss is supervisor of the Mushroom Green Chainshop, and chairs the Industrial Archaeological Group of the Black Country Society.

Dry Cooperage

Ralph Smith

In 1840, at the age of eleven, Thomas Smith of Quarry Bank began his apprenticeship with Edward Tinsley to learn the trade of coopering. Eleven years later he married Elizabeth Trevis and they set up home in Newtown, Cradley Heath. At the age of 51, in 1880, he left the employ of Edward Tinsley to establish his own cooperage business. He produced both "wet cooperage", to hold liquids, and "dry cooperage" which was used for packing purposes. His son, Thomas Trevis-Smith, acquired land in what became Holly Bush Street, and the cooper's shop was established there. Thomas Trevis-Smith died in 1911, leaving his 19-year-old son, Ernest, to run the business, joined in 1913 by brother Bertram. Soon afterwards wet cooperage declined as part of their business and dry cooperage and diversification became the order of the day. Ernest Smith's son, Ralph, was born in 1920, and it is his account of his working life, which is still continuing, that is produced here. (In 1980 Thomas Trevis Smith Ltd. produced a centenary booklet detailing the history of the business.)

I started work in 1934 at the age of fourteen, I think it was automatic that the son went into the father's business, it just seemed a pre-ordained course that I had to follow, and I think that happened to everybody at that time. At first I worked three days a week and attended Technical School for two days, but later I attended the Technical School on three evenings. I studied engineering and draughtsmanship and quite a wide range of things as there were no specialist courses in cooperage.

As far as I can remember the first job I had to do was stacking staves. The oak staves, about 24 inches long had to be stored in stacks that seemed sky high, and they were left to dry out for three or four months. I also had to deliver casks to the local chainworks like Hingley's, Griff's and N.B.Homer. I had to carry a cask under each arm on half mile trips - and I've still got the scars to prove it! It was painful when the casks rubbed your skin. All deliveries at the time were made on foot, although we did have a six foot long barrow to carry half a dozen casks at a time if necessary.

I also had to help in the yard, cutting staves, and in 1940 I lost a finger doing that. Sometimes ten tons of oak staves, already cut, would come in on a lorry from a supplier in Stafford and I would have to stack them, which would keep me busy for a couple of weeks. To obtain ash we would make a trip into the Worcestershire countryside. Ash in diameter between 1 and 8" was available from small trees. The 1 was grown from stools (the base of a tree that has been coppiced) and the timber was quartered to make wooden hoops, after being shaved, steam-bent into a coil, and left to dry and set.

Ralph Smith demonstrates a machine devised at Trevis Smith Ltd., to make a wooden lid for a cask in one operation (Photo: Ned Williams)

Left: Bertram Smith and Rupert Kilvert outside the office, in the yard at 38 Holly Bush Street, Cradley Heath, about 1930.

Right: A picture of Ralph Smith as a very young child showing a very early interest in cooperage. (Company's collection)

Half our trade consisted of making casks, and the other half consisted of making packing cases. I was able to make packing cases early in my career, knocking them up with hammer and nails. It is difficult to imagine now how many items were packed in dry casks. We supplied many to the edge tool trade, to companies like John Perks at Monmore Green, and Brades of Oldbury. Hoes, for example, could be packed in casks, packed in spirals supporting each other until the cask was almost filled solid with steel. But greater use of tractors has led to a decline in the once vast export of hoes.

Casks are ideal packing because you can put half a ton in a cask, lie it on its side and roll it anywhere you like - even up two planks and onto a cart with no problem, but if you put half a ton in a packing case you can't shift it. You put it on the ground and it stays there! But what killed our trade was the advent of the fork-lift truck. Packing cases then really came into their own and we still make them today.

My electrical and mechanical engineering knowledge began to come in useful in maintaining the machines we were gradually introducing into the business. By the time I was twenty I started building machines, and some of them are still working today. You can't buy coopering machinery - you have to adapt or make your own. It is so specialised that if a machine is built it tends to be a "one off". We have bought machines from other cooperages as they have closed down over the years. They have vanished to such an extent that the nearest one to us is now in Manchester!

Our machines were originally powered by a gas engine (an 8hp machine built by National Gas) with a long shaft with flat belts driving two saws and a planing machine. The belts were always breaking so I eventually changed to rubber V belts. I used to help the sawyer man to start the engine first thing each morning, and on cold mornings it was a pig to start. We eventually broke up the gas engine when we moved to our present premises - it would be a real museum piece now!

During the early part of the War I learnt how to make casks, but by then fifty percent of the work was

done by machine so it was not difficult. I still made deliveries but by then we had a lorry, so I spent a couple of years lorry driving and kept my HGV licence until I was 65. In fact I think I've done every job on the ground from book-keeping to digging and laying drains. Everybody who works here has to be flexible, but I think that is what makes life pleasant. I'm sure it's much more interesting if work is full of variety.

About 1941/42 we started using steel hoops. We used steel strip that came into the country on bales of cotton from Egypt. I made a machine to splay the strip - shaping it to fit the contour of the barrel. Some of our customers did not like such innovations. For example the Post Office Telephones, to whom we supplied thousands of casks insisted on still having wooden hoops, despite the fact that over the following fifteen years it became more and more difficult to obtain the wood and to make them. Our last wooden-hoop-maker died a fortnight ago, and now that is a trade that has vanished. We had to make a gunpowder barrel for a museum the other day and I had to fly wooden hoops in from France because I don't think there is anybody left in this country who can make them.

The staves had to be cut down to their tapered shape at each end, by using an upturned plane called a jointer, and the sides had to be bevelled off at the same time, also with a plane. We have found ways of doing this by machine, and we have even put a cutter in the planing machine that does all the hollowing and backing, that gives the staves the right shape to form the wall of cask. In the old cooperage trade it was done with what was called a "horse", and it was a long painstaking job. The horse was a sloping piece of timber with a swinging gate on it which traps the timber as you shave it. I'm sure we've still got one somewhere.

During the War we made some tubs for the Ministry of Supply, similar to those used by the Navy for the Rum Issue, but ours were for the storage of salted meat. They were made of first class oak to wet cooperage standards, and when we had finished we had a huge pile of oak staves left over. What could we do with them? I thought I'll make a dozen plant tubs. I took them over to an Uncle who had a nursery at Hagley.

"I'll never sell those in a blue moon," he said, "they don't want to pay for the plant, never mind for a tub as well. You don't stand an earthly, but you can put 'em out, and we'll give 'em a run."

A week later he telephoned,

"Ralph, have you got any more of those tubs - they've all gone!"

So we used up all the surplus staves, and we have never stopped making plant tubs ever since! Between July and Christmas we have to make ten thousand Christmas Tree tubs. It illustrates the way we have diversified and survived largely by accident. Other aspects of the business have developed in the same way, for example storage and garden furniture.

The warehousing and storage had started at our old premises. They were typical of many Black Country business premises having expanded over the years by buying the house next door, the shed on one side, and a yard on another etc. In the end we found we had acquired 15000 square feet of which we only wanted half the area - and so we went into storage.

In the case of garden furniture, we took over a Birmingham firm, an old cooper which had been going since the last century, and they had diversified into garden furniture. We carried it on, and have never stopped. We have changed direction completely, from industrial packaging to making non-essential luxury items. We do still make pallets and packing cases but it is probably less than a third of our business. We used to supply one firm with three lorry-loads a day of packing cases but they suddenly closed down and, overnight, that trade was gone. That's why we diversify and that's why we have to be flexible.

We'll do anything in timber as long as it's not joinery, for the simple reason that if you are in the packing trade business and you start making joinery two things can happen and both are disastrous: you either get joinery made like packing cases or packing cases made like joinery! We do still get asked to make barrels and casks because there is nobody else left to do it. We have just made a cask for Jim Hawkins to hide in for the new Charlton Heston film of "Treasure Island". We used ash hoops that were forty years old that we still had in stock! And we've been making tankards from the timber salvaged from the wreck of HMS Invincible that sank in the Solent in 1759.

We have never had a great deal of staff turnover. Many people have been with us for years and we work together on a friendly basis. I'd rather establish a family atmosphere than make a pile of money. I want to enjoy myself and have a happy life. I enjoy my work, that's why I decided to go on working rather than pack it up ten years ago. If somebody enjoys playing golf, he should go and play. If somebody enjoys working he should go on working. The human being has to do something, and if we hadn't got work it would have to be invented. Even the caveman started doing something to fill his time in.

I like the challenge of doing different things, something different all the while. I like to please myself and I'm glad I've had the freedom that comes of working for yourself even if sometimes there are restrictions of time and finance. I look back fondly to the days during the War when my Uncle and I often worked till midnight every night to keep the machines working. In the last year or two younger members of the family have come in and developed our marketing, something we never had time for in the old days. Consequently the long battle we have been through to replace our cask and packing case work has paid off, and the horticultural products have "taken off". My basic point is that we'll have a go at anything in wood, and we are not afraid of change.

Staff and products of Thos. Trevis Smith Ltd., celebrating the centenary of the business in 1980, on the present site at Portersfield Road. Products displayed include casks, packing cases, plant tubs, and wheel barrows. (Company's collection)

Brick kilns like this were once a common sight in the Black Country. A few survived into the 1980's at Oak Lane, Pensnett, and are now oil–fired. (BCS Collection)

The Firebrick Trade

Sid Wooldridge

After I left school I had one or two jobs until finishing up in the sheet metal industry, making things like dustbins, and I was very happy in that trade. Then one Monday morning we went to work to find the boss waiting there to meet us, saying, "Don't take your coats off - You won't work here again!" We were rather puzzled, and thought we had done something wrong, but it turned out that the firm had gone into liquidation. Due to the level of unemployment at that time we were all out of work for the next eighteen months.

Finally, in 1932, at the age of eighteen, I was offered a job in the firebrick works as a "page", as they were called in those days. I had to work with a master brick-maker, rolling the clay for him and assisting him. At that time Bowens Refactories had just gone into the making of fire backs. These were hand moulded and it was quite a good trade. I graduated to being a moulder two years before the War. I registered for the RAMC but was told that I was in a reserved occupation so I had to remain in the firebrick industry, although we stopped making grate backs and had to concentrate on furnace linings.

The work was very heavy and the conditions in which we worked were very primitive - even the drive into the works was just an unsurfaced cart-track. We had no gas, no electricity, no canteen, no facilities to make anything. Although the company used water in the boiler any water that we used in the course of our work had to be fetched from the cut!

The actual place I worked in was called a "stow". It was a brick-built building with a hollow floor. Beneath the floor were channels, and at the end of the building these channels led to hearths where fires were pushed in. The heat passed under the foor, to dry the bricks, and passed up the stack at the other end of the building. Winter time was the worst because we had to prevent the frost entering the clay and the building had to be filled with smoke fires. These were just old buckets with holes knocked round them, like a roadmender's brazier, and the fire was put into them - not a red glowing fire, but rather a smoke, which killed the frost. In this smoke you could be working at a table with a pal and you wouldn't be able to see him for the smoke.

The process of making bricks began at the steam driven mill. This was a huge contraption with two revolving wheels running on a pan which had a surface like a grating. The clay was ground and dropped through onto a an endless belt which took it up onto a screen, at the top of which it was sieved to the right grade. Once sieved it fell into a huge pan in which two huge blades rotated to mix the clay. A chap above the pan ran a hosepipe of water into it to bring it to the right consistency - he was called the "temperer".

We worked with clay mixed with ground up waste fire bricks.

At the bottom of the mill was another chap who dropped the clay into barrows which were wheeled to the brickmakers. It was impossible to get every barrow of clay to the same strength so sometimes it was very soft, other times it was too hard to punch. Another problem was that you didn't want the clay to dry out, so you had to get Hurden bags (Hessian sacks) and spread them out on your floorspace and sprinkle them with water to keep them damp while your clay was tipped out. Some days you had to work with thirty barrows of clay.

There were two kinds of moulding process: wet moulding and dry moulding. In wet moulding you made your brick on the floor, which was uneven, with an open wooden mould - there was no bottom in it. The clay had to be very soft, and the clods were rolled on the floor to make sure there were no air cavities in the clay. You had to throw your clay into the mould, the secret being not to let the clay catch the side of the mould. when the mould was filled you cut off the top surplus with a quaint contraption like a cheese cutter called a "bow". With the water you had fetched from the canal you wet a wooden straight edge to level the brick off. When you had done that you had to draw the mould up - hoping the mould would not stick. Later you went round with a knife to cut off any waste and then left the brick on the floor to dry out to a nice dark colour. You had to judge when it was firm enough to be straightened with a scythe blade and when you could lift it onto its side and drop it onto a flat board to scrape the bottom. In this way we might make up to forty 24"x24"x3" bricks a day.

Dry moulding used a mould with a bottom in it, although the sides might be removable. It was a way of making bricks of particular shapes as used in a furnace. The clay had to be firmer, and after it was dropped into the mould you had to punch it with your fists to fill all the corners of the mould. When full the mould would have to be "bumped", maybe twenty times, to completely settle the clay. The brick had to be turned out of the mould very carefully.

At the right time the setters came with their barrows and took the bricks out of your stow and set them up in kilns. The kilns were round in shape, with domed tops, and were fired by coal. Sometimes they burned for a fortnight. At the beginning of the process the bricks still had to be dried out so a smoking fire was used for the first three or four days until, when you looked up you couldn't see any steam coming from the top of the stack. As long as you could see steam you knew there was still damp in the bricks. The kiln-burner was a very skilled man with keen eyesight and a wealth of experience.

The women moulders made the small bricks - like housebricks in size. They always did wet moulding (in their case we called it slop moulding), and the conditions in which they worked were pathetic. They had very hot floors, and they worked round a table by a water bosh. After making the mould really wet they put it on a slab to make the brick (We called it a "slob"). They had to get the brick off the slab, carrying two or three bricks at a time to the floor, and running back to carry on. In some cases their "stent" for a day's work was a thousand bricks. You never saw their faces - all you saw were slits for their eyes. Their faces and chests were covered with clay and running with water. Other women were in setting gangs - carrying bricks to the kilns. They used to get a bag, stuff it with straw, tie it round their waist and would rest the bricks, perhaps eight at a time, on this apron. Like the men, most were heavy drinkers and smokers because there was so much dust in the atmosphere, although it could also be smokey and damp. I smoked sixty cigarettes a day while I worked in the brickyard and I reckon that it saved my life. Of course we were always getting brick dust out of each others eyes, because as you tipped your mould over, all the dust came up in your face. But the clay kept your hands very clean and soft!

There were two rates of pay - Day work or tonnage. We called the former "Stent" work and if you were dry moulding you had to agree a price with the manager defining how many bricks would be considered a day's work. Wet moulding was paid on the tonnage principle based on the weight of the bricks you had produced after they had been burnt. Although none of us had a good education we had to be good at reckoning up to check that we were being paid correctly. And there were many injustices in the system.

After the War we started a branch of the General and Municipal Workers Union to try and improve wages and conditions but it was a difficult trade in which to negotiate, partly bcause it was all so primitive. I worked at Bowen's yard at Brettle Lane for thirty five years and by the time I finished we had five weeks holiday a year, a canteen, and a guaranteed week. Rather different from Wartime when sometimes you could struggle to work for three days running, and not earn a penny if the boss told you there was no clay or the mill had broken down. After the War I returned to making grate backs and it was a trade that did good business.

There was a good feeling of comradeship amongst brickyard workers - we were all very down-to-earth Black Country people - interested in whippets and gambling. If an older worker had a hernia operation a good foreman could usually give him some lighter work paging for someone else for a few weeks. Unfortunatley, in my mid fifties, I had to face an operation and when I returned to the brickyard I found a new foreman had arrived. I asked him if I could have light work for a few weeks but he said, "Sid, where the bloody hell is light work in a brickworks? I dunno what we can do." I said, "That's all right, I'll have my cards."

Making Glass

C.W.Harper

I suppose it was inevitable that as I was eldest son of a glassmaker and the grandson of a skilled glass cutter, that I should follow in their footsteps and become a glassmaker. I had won a scholarship to the Stourbridge School of Art at the age of fourteen, where glassmaking was one of the subjects taught. All phases of glassmaking were taught, including design, manufacture and decoration. As a matter of fact, in 1935, it was said to be the only school in the world which catered for glassmaking. The department was in the basement of the school, in Church Street, Stourbridge. The teacher in glassmaking was a Mr. Charles Stanier and the Decorating teacher was a Mr. Webb. I was there for a full two years, daytime and evenings as well.

We learned the basic steps of gathering the glass on a hot iron, which was placed in the furnace and then turned with the fingers round one way from left to right so that the molten glass stuck to it. After that we were taught how to gather the glass on a blowing iron, a hollow steel tube, which allowed one to blow down the cold end to shape the glass at the hot end. In that way it was possible to make a shape either by hand or in a mould. As our skill increased we used more molten glass until we could blow large pieces.

My father had always wanted to have his own factory making glass, and had the hope that if his sons became glassmakers that is what he would do. We all worked for Thos. Webb & Sons in Amblecote. I started at the age of sixteen, in 1937, and worked a fixed shift of six hours and six hours off, from Monday to Friday. My father worked that way from 1922 to 1939 - always on the same shifts. I worked from six to twelve in the morning and then returned to work from six till midnight the same day.

It was hard work in front of furnaces that had a temperature of 1300' centigrade and one's social life was non-existant for five days. Then the War came and that was the end of the shift, "six off-six on" as it was known. Because of the Blackout all windows had to be shut at night and even shutters had to be made to make sure that no light escaped. The shifts were altered to six till two, and two till ten, which was a pleasant surprise for the glassmakers because they were able to socialize after work during the week for the first time. They could go for a drink of beer at night instead of drinking it at work. Drinking at work was always allowed because it was so hot and you were sweating all the time. Some sweated more than others, and drank more than others, but I have seen sweat run from the shoes of people while at work, and the next day they had dried white with salt that the sweat had soaked from the leather.

I became a glassblower at the furnace not long after starting work. With training and hard work I progressed to being a glassmaker and a "gaffer" of my "chair". That meant that I was boss of the team, usually consisting of five or six men and boys. A lot of us kept our teams for a few years, until the younger ones progressed up the ladder, and were replaced by new boys. Everyone worked on a piecework basis.

The difficult part of glassmaking, of course, is that you have to learn to work the hot glass into shape while it is still hot, which means that you can't hang about. You only have a few seconds to shape it before it becomes set. Working piecework also sets the pace, and I have made as many as five hundred wine glasses for a day's work. They are always graded into firsts and seconds, and the more firsts you have made - the better your wages. Sometimes the glass would not melt as well as at other times and it would be difficult to make as many firsts so your wages suffered. We were also working as a team and could be affected by one member of the team not feeling too good, maybe suffering a hang over from too much beer the night before.

When I started work my first week's wage was 18/6, which today is 92 pence. I gave my mother 13/6 (67p) for my keep, leaving me five shillings for myself (25p). There were seven of us in the family and as I was the eldest I was the first to go to work, so very often I would give my mother a shilling (5p) of my "pocket money" in the middle of the week to buy some meat as the house-keeping money would have gone by then.

I carried on working throughout the War years because most of us were on reserved occupations and were not asked to do military service. I did volunteer for the RAF, and passed the medical and the tests, but was not allowed to go, because the work we did was part of the War Effort. When the War ended the shutters over the windows in the glasshouse were taken down and we could see the sky again while we were working.

After the War had finished I was offered a job in Hertfordshire at a glassworks called Nazeing Glass. I stayed there for ten years and I learned quite a lot of different methods of glassmaking because most of the people who were skilled were foreigners with different ways of doing things. After ten years I came back to Amblecote - back to Thos. Webb & Co. to work there as a glassmaker until I retired two years ago, after being in the trade for forty nine years.

During that time many things changed in the industry. Chiefly the conditions improved: it's not quite as dirty as it used to be. There is also more time off for holidays. When I started there was no Holiday Pay so you saved your half crown a week in the Holiday club, which, in fifty weeks gave you the princely sum of £6 5s with which to go on holiday. After the War we were granted one week's Holiday Pay, and from the mid-fifties onwards we were given two weeks.

Glassmaking can be frustrating if the team is not working effectively. Sometimes the "boy", the youngest member of the team who has just started requires a lot of teaching, or might be a bit awkward with his hands. If he turned out to be left-handed, what we called caggy-handed, he had to be taught to be right-handed, as everything is done that way. I have only ever seen one left-handed blower, and he had to work alone! The satisfaction of glassmaking is the knowledge that you have created something with your own hands and your own skill which gives you pleasure, and brings pleasure to the person who buys it.

Different ways of making articles in glass have emerged but a great many of the old skills are still used. You can still say that Stourbridge Glass is truly Hand Made.

Working at Chance's

John and Eunice Horton

In 1841 one and a quarter million square feet of glass were used in the construction of the Crystal Palace. In 1951 the Science Exhibition at the Festival of Britain was glazed with a new pattern "Festival" glass. On each occasion the glass was made by the same company - Chance Brothers, Spon Lane, Smethwick. The company was established in Spon Lane in 1824 in an old 15 acre glassworks. It grew until it occupied 40 acres and employed approximately 3000 workers. In this account John Horton describes his engineering apprenticeship at Chance's and Eunice recalls her work as a comptometer operator:

I started my apprenticeship at Chance Brothers on 16th September 1946, having been sent there by the Careers people in Birmingham. I lived in Stourbridge so one of the most significant aspects of starting work was having to get up at six in the morning to catch the 6.35. from Stourbridge Junction. The very first winter I started work was the bad winter of 1947 - there was no heating on in the factory and the trains were crowded, but the chief consolation was that the 6.35. started from Bewdley and the coaches were warm by the time I joined the train. With a bit of luck I could run to Smethwick Junction, having finished work at five, and catch a train at nine minutes past five and be home for tea by half past five!

I first worked in the Fitting Shop, and in the little section that I worked in we made incandescent lamps in which vaporized paraffin was burnt in a mantle to give thousands of candlepower of light once inside a lighthouse optic. We also made multi-wick lamps for bouys and quay lamps. They were like large blow lamps. We started with a brass sheet and rolled them up and brazed them. I received my training while engaged in production work - I must have made about 100,000 blow lamp prickers while I was an apprentice, and we made things like valves for the top of gas bottles for BOC. Lighthouse construction was as much a matter of engineering as it was about optics and glass.

We learnt the jobs by the older hands showing us how to do things. That would be frowned on today because it was a way of passing on mistakes, but most people at Chances had worked at the firm for years and were very experienced. If you were helping them on a piecework job you got a thump if you didn't do something correctly. The charge hand was 79 and had been at Chance's since 1894, but generally I enjoyed the company of the people I worked with and the work itself was interesting.

Like all apprentices, I was sent for a long weight at the stores, but because I had stayed at school until I was sixteen I was a bit wiser than some of the young lads. We had a day off a week to go to Tech, where we developed a separate circle of friends, and I can't help thinking that generally we were more "able" than today's apprentices. Chance Technical College, in Crocketts Lane, had been founded by Chance Brothers and the company had always been interested in education and training. One of the few buildings that survives today is the old school building that Chances had erected in 1845 for the education of employees' children.

Harold Gough (right), the Chief Lighthouse Engineer, inspects the work of Fred Ashley, the Optic Fitter, at Chance Brothers, Spon Lane, Smethwick, in 1951. (John Horton's collection)

Our lighthouse products went all over the world and our largest customers were the Crown Agents, for the Commonwealth, and Trinity House for home sales. We were replacing equipment that had been damaged or neglected during the War. We made big weight-driven clocks to drive lighthouses where no power was available, and even spiral staircases to go in lighthouses. We built bouy lights which had mechanisms like musical boxes to give them their flash characteristics, and, of course, we made diaphones, better known as fog horns.

The fog horns had to be tuned up, and the organist from Pedmore Church, another veteran employee of the firm, had to blow his reed pipe to check that they were in tune. When we tested fog signals they were sometimes heard as far away as Kidderminster!

After leaving the Fitting Shop I went to the Electrical Shop where we made brazing torches and all sorts of things like stand-by generators for the Post Office. After twelve months of that I went into the Machine Shop and mainly worked on Capstan lathes, which I enjoyed. I did small runs of sixty or seventy components, but it is the setting up which is the interesting thing on capstans.

Then I went in the office to learn production control. I did a lot of costing and estimating, and also got involved with work study and time study in the glass grinding shop where we ground the prisms for lighthouse optics - it all came back to glass in the end. The glass was cast in the glassworks and arrived as a rough bent prism. It was bedded on some pitch on some very crude and ancient machines. They were revolved and two cast iron rubbers rubbed the glass. A handful of coarse carborundum was chucked on, and as the process went on this became finer and finer. Eventually felt pads polished the glass with ruitile. At the same time the angles had to be right so that the light would refract through the prism correctly.

There were so many things we made out of glass - from glass balls for sunshine recorders to microscope slides. Although training as an engineer I gradually saw more and more of the glass production - from seeing the cullet (broken glass used in the mix) arriving by canal boat to the casting, blowing, and cutting of glass. I used to travel to work on the train with the man who made the fireclay pots in which glass was cast. He used to tread the clay himself to get it to the right consistency. Sometimes the production methods were surprising - for example microscope slides were blown. I big bubble was blown and spun until it flattened out. It was then cracked to leave a big four foot diameter disc of glass only ten thou thick and girls would then cut it up into little rectangles to make slides.

Many jobs required great experience and skill, and, as I've said many people stayed at Chance's all their lives. I probably thought I would stay until I retired. The lighthouse engineer himself was in his eighties. I worked with a Mr. Hipkins who had been there for years in the Estimating Section. When we recieved an order he would say, "Ah, we made one of those in 1898 - if you look in book four you'll find it on page 41." In my time estimates were still done in indelible pencil on a piece of paper which was then put in the ledger with a damp cloth and pressed until it was printed there.

Our blacksmith was an old chap named Len Kettle. He used to make the large single point tools for the lathes and the boring machines. He had an apprentice to strike for him, and his famous saying was, "When I nod my head, hit it!" One day the apprentice missed the hot steel and the 14lb hammer bounced off the anvil and hit Len on the forehead, and knocked him into the water bosh.

My apprenticeship finished on 26th June 1951 and I then became eligble for call up. I joined the Army in April 1952. While I was away Chance's was taken over by Pilkingtons who disposed of the engineering side to Stones of Deptford. When my National Service was completed in the summer of 1954 I went to Lucas as a work study engineer.

Eunice Horton: I left school at Christmas 1950 and went to a comptometer school for three months. They sent me to Chance's for an interview. I had never worked anywhere else or knew any different so it seemed all right to me. I started work in the Wages Office on 23rd April 1951.

The work was calculating wages from the time sheets and adding the wages sheets up, and I did that for about three years. Then they wanted someone to go and work on Fridays in the Lighthouse Department, which I did until that side was taken over by Stones. I also had some experience of calculating wages in the Blowing and Pressing Department. The point was that each department had a different way of calculating wages. Some were on piecework, in others a price was neghotiated for the job itself. Another time I worked three days a week in the Cost Office doing a variety of work, costing and checking invoices

A comptometer is an adding and calculating machine, and the school had trained me in all its operations, including how to get a reciprocal. I found being a comptometer operator interesting because I like machines, but not typewriters, and I like working with numbers. In a wages office you have to get everything done by a certain time so there is a bit of a challenge. In that office I worked with one other comptometer operator and eleven wages clerks and an office manager.

Chance's was a very sociable place to work, and I joined in the social side of things and played netball for the works team, played badminton and went to dances. Even with 3,000 employees they managed to create a family atmosphere. Hugh Chance himself was a real gentleman, and at Christmas he walked around the works and wished every he met a Happy Christmas and shook their hand.

Rolled plate glass was produced by Chance Brothers at Spon Lane by an automatic continuous process. In this picture the glass is being cut to size at the end of the annealing lehr. 1955. (Sandwell Public Libraries & Museums)

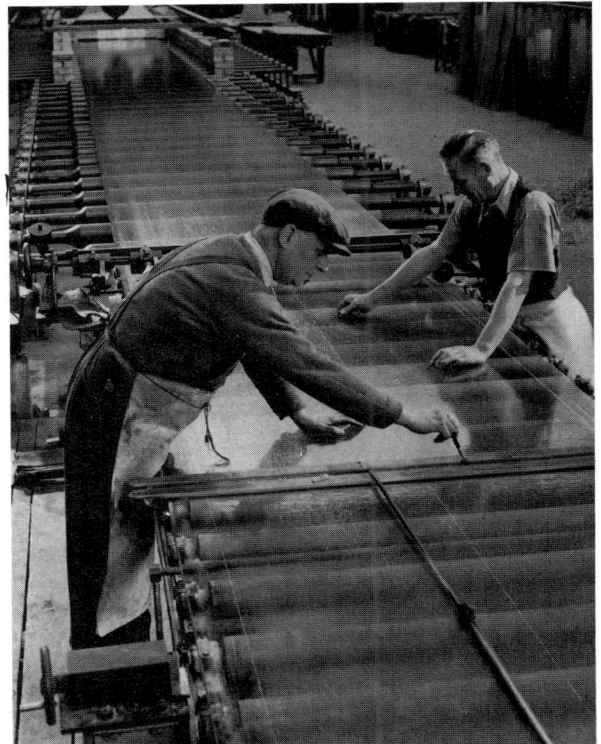

One of the Lead Burners

Charlie Price

I was a lead burner, and not many people know what a lead burner is. In fact when I was called up during the War they didn't know what it was and that it was a reserved occupation. One of my colleagues, who had been in the T.A. slipped into the Army and the company was still trying to get him back by the time he was in North Africa!

I started work at Chance & Hunt, Oldbury (later ICI), in 1928. I was fourteen and had come straight from school. At first I worked in the Time Office as an errand boy until I was sixteen and it was decided what I should do next. I wanted to be a carpenter, but there were no spare places to train as a carpenter. They suggested that I be bricklayer but that conjured up a picture of stuggling up a ladder with a heavy hod full of bricks, so I settled to be a plumber instead. Little did I realise that lead was far heavier than bricks!

So, at the age of sixteen, I went off to the Plumbing Shop to become a chemical plumber or a lead burner. At first I was just the tea boy, fetching things, carrying the lead burners' tools to where they were working, sweeping up and cleaning the workshop windows, and lighting the fires. I was allowed to practice working with lead and welding it in any spare moments, but sometimes I managed to do it for two or three hours between my other duties. I had a natural feeling for it, and once they saw I was all right I was given little jobs to do. For example I had to make boxes - and if they had no real use they could be melted down and the lead used again.

Eventually I went out on jobs. Sometimes when I was working in very awkward places I found it was necessary to weld left-handed. One day the foreman saw me doing this and said, "Who taught you to weld left-handed?"
"Nobody," I replied, "I taught myself."
I also had to go to night school, which I had to pay for myself, where I learnt such things as reading drawings. One class started at 5.30., and as we did not finish work until five, I was often late. The lecturer threatened me with expulsion but I told him what I thought of him and persuaded him to talk to the Oldbury Works and ask that I leave work earlier. The matter was settled by the college being persuaded to allow me to arrive late!

Once I could read drawings I was able to mark out the lead and prepare it for cutting. We marked it out by coating a string with chalk and twanging it against the lead to mark the line. It was cut with a burner specially designed for working with lead - with a small jet. Lead in sheet form was measured by its weight per square yard. For example if we worked in 6lb. lead, one square foot of it would weigh 6lb. We used sheets that were 8ft. by 4ft. so you can see they were very heavy.

The Leadburners: From left to right – Mr. Kilpatrick, the foreman, Charlie Price, Tommy Tromans, Sammy Hadley, Ron Fellows and Ted Wilson. Back Row from right – Jim Croft plus two unidentified labourers. On the table is a variety of objects made in lead forming part of an exhibition and open day put on by Chance & Hunt in the early fifties - note the shield and elaborate rainhead. Charlie Price is wearing ex-Police trousers issued to the workers by Chance & Hunt as hard-wearing working clothes. (Charlie Price's collection)

The Leadburners at work: putting the top on a lead chamber – the towers in which acids were produced – at the works of Chance & Hunt, Oldbury, in the early fifties, looking across to the Rowley Hills. From left to right: Bill Hart, Sammy Hadley, Ted Wilson, Charlie Price in his hard hat, and unidentified assistant. The lead walls of the chamber can just be seen at the front of the picture. (Charlie Price's collection)

As lead burners we formed a team that built tanks and the chambers in which the acids were made. The chamber in which the sulphuric acid was produced was 76ft.4in. high and 32ft.6ins. diameter. There were landings at 7ft.6ins. intervals all the way up and there were six such towers in the plant - making other acids besides the sulphuric acid. It took about six weeks to build a chamber and they ran for about eighteen months before they would be shut down and rebuilt. The sulphuric acid boiling away inside these tanks only occupied the bottom eighteen inches of the tank - the rest was gas through which water fell to produce the acid.

The lead sheets had to welded together in an upright position and we did this work in all weathers. In the snow we used to protect ourselves by hanging a railway tarpaulin from one of the landings, but I enjoyed the work - I always liked building anything. In the winter of '47 the water running down the outside of the towers formed huge three foot long icicles!

Lead was also used to line the inside of the company's tankers. As I was the thinnest I had to get inside the tanker to do the lead burning. When I came out I stank to high heaven! While working in there I had to have a rope tied round my waist. The other end of the rope was held by the labourer standing outside. If there was any trouble you were supposed to pull on the rope - which was fine as long as the labourer had not gone to sleep.

From sometime before the War we had worked with plastic - and welding the plastic together was very similar to working with lead. Despite the fact that we had been familiar with plastic for years someone after the War decided that me and Tommy Tromans, a real Black Country lad from Blackheath, should go on a "refresher course". As it would be a day out we agreed to go. The experts were showing us how to weld plastic

together and all the big bugs were sitting there watching. Suddenly Tommy shouted out, "Good God, Charlie, look at the bloody arse he's got on the end of there!" It was an expression we used to describe a bulge in the plastic, but everybody was disgusted. The demonstrator said, "If you can do any better, come up here and do it."

Tommy replied, "If we couldn't do better than that we'd been out of a job years ago!" And then we showed them how to do it.

I worked all my life at Chance & Hunt, leaving in 1965 after thirty seven years service. I became quite familiar with long service awards. I received a silver watch after 20 years and a lady's gold wrist watch, which I gave to my daughter, after 25 years. As I approached thirty years service I was serving on the Works Council so I said to the Council, "Surely a bloke has got a bloody watch by the time we are presenting him with one." I persuaded the council that an employee should choose his own gift and have something that he and his wife could share in their home. The Manager and I had to go up to Liverpool to persuade all the ICI of this idea, the folks from Wednesbury, Widnes, Wigan, Fleetwood and so on. I proposed the idea and my manager seconded it, and it was passed.

Having given the 25 year gold watch to my daughter, I decided to give my 20 year silver watch to my son. He was working as a chef in Birmingham and one day he came home from work and said, "I am sorry, Dad, but I've lost your watch." A fortnight later he rang to say it had been found - at the bottom of the stock pot. The watch had boiled in the stock for two weeks. It had stopped and seemed in rather a sorry state so my wife took it to a jeweller. "Blimey," he said, "what have you been doing with this? - it looks as if it's been in the soup!" But he cleaned it up and it still keeps perfect time to this day.

Ron Hawkins demonstrates the art of finishing and dressing leather at Walsall Leather Museum, May 1989. He is showing how a currier would have "set out" a bridle butt using a stainless steel slicker - the kind of tool that curriers usually made for themselves as they learnt their trade. (Photo: Sarah Wood)

A Life in Leather

Ron Hawkins

As a fourteen-year-old school leaver in 1940 I had briefly worked in the metal trade but my hands were allergic to the slurry oil, so I decided to go for leather. I suppose it was natural for me to look for a job in the leather trade as my grandfather had worked at Boak's as a boilerman. He had often taken me there as a child and I had always displayed great interest when I was shown round. I was also fascinated by the legend that no four-legged animal ever ran down Holden's yard and ever came out alive. They would have the skin off its back and would tan it - such was their dedication to tanning. What was a fact was that E.T.Holden was the first leather factory to open a tannery in Walsall way back in 1819. I applied to them and they accepted me as a trainee.

I started, like all the other boys in the firm, in the warehouse. This entailed jobs such as sweeping-up, fetching and running errands, and delivering parcels of leather to, various firms in the town that were supplied by E.T.Holden. They were very famous manufacturers of high quality pig skins and the enamelled, or Japanned leather, which was also known as patent leather. To a lesser extent they also supplied bridle, harness and equestrian leathers, and, in later years, clothing leather. The firm did not have mechanical transport in those days to make deliveries so that was a job that was done by the boys, and, at any one time, there would always be at least three boys in the warehouse.

Eventually we were designated to other parts of the factory to learn the basis of different jobs. By then our warehouse experience had taught us about the different kinds of leathers as well as how to pack it for sale and export. We gradually obtained an overall view of what went on in the factory and slowly began to specialise. For example, some went into the Finishing Department, where the colour was applied, some went into splitting and shaving the leather, and others went into the tannery. That was not a very popular

choice as it was very smelly work and the process was all done by hand, and it was very cold in winter.

I was designated to be trained as a currier, which was a highly skilled job in those days. I was trained by some of the older men at the firm, most of whom had been doing it all their lives. Many had over fifty years experience, and one chap was eighty four! The training was supposed to take several years but the War had come along and much of the traditional training was dispensed with. A shortage of manpower affected the firm as men went away to War. My brother and even my mother came to work at Holden's. It had always been a very male-dominated trade but women came in to do some of the lighter work, and, in fact, my mother was the last woman to leave after the War. They had to ask her to leave as she was the only woman left - not that it mattered to her, as she liked leather work so much!

I served in the RAF for four years but was able to return to Holden's in 1947 to continue my training as a currier until the management decided I was competent. Once I became a fully fledged currier I carried on in that capacity until 1955. In that year the boss, Mr.Thomas Holden-White Snr. suddenly died, and at about the same time we lost a man called George Payton. He had been a very knowledgeable leather worker and we all believed his War experiences must have brought about his early death. I was offered his job, and the new boss, Mr.Thomas Holden-White Jnr. told me that his father, before he had died, had already decided that I was to be given the job if anything happened to George. So I found myself promoted to the staff. I had to sort and grade the pig skins, oversee customers' orders, see to their despatch, and see that the job progressed reasonably through our factory. The post didn't really have a name because in the leather trade there was no tradition of one man only knowing one job. In other words you were always prepared to do whatever job you were asked to do, and titles didn't seem to matter.

There were Heads of Departments - Enamelling, General Work, Light Work - and really I was in charge of the latter. Every morning we were summoned to the office by the boss, after the mail had been sorted, and each "Head" was given his allocation of orders for the day. Some orders could be met from stock, some had to be put into production from scratch. It was our job to get the work done, see it through the factory, check it and grade it and see that the hides were measured before despatch. Some hides were sold by the square foot, others were sold by the piece. I felt some trepidation about going into the job but I was extremely keen to do it - and I enjoyed wearing clean clothes for a change! This was a perticularly welcome change because leather work is such a dirty job, as a result of using oils, greases, dyes, and horrible chemicals like ammonia and formaldahide and borax. Our clothes just seemed to stink.

I had often heard people say, "Where there's muck - there's brass," - well, we saw plenty of the muck but not much of the brass. My first week's wages, as a boy of seventeen, was seven and ninepence (38p) - one good weekend and your pocket money had gone! However, I made progress and was eventually promoted to foreman and then to senior foreman. I was really an assistant, or understudy, to the Works Manager and was promised that one day I would have that position. It did not work out that way.

In the mid sixties E.T.Holden decided that they would sell their town-centre site in Park Street and take over an abandoned tannery near the Walsall Arboretum. The move was accomplished over a year in which we moved a few pieces of equipment at a time or duplicated equipment on both sites so that production could be maintained throughout the transition. The doors at the Park Street premises closed in August 1967 and the former Greatrex's tannery in Leicester Street became fully operational. The company stayed there until 1970 when it was decided to move the whole business to Scotland. They already owned a tannery in Jedburgh, and had bought an old woollen mill in the same town - and it was decided that we move the firm into that building.

We had a full order book and had just installed new equipment in Walsall - we were more productive than we had ever been so it was a great shock when I was eventually told about the move. I was told that merging with the operation in Jedburgh would cut costs and that there were advantages in moving to a development area that badly needed industry. I decided to accept redundancy and look for another position.

I had thirty years experience in the trade and knew local firms well. I was offered jobs at Sedgewicks, Underwoods, and Boak. The last two have since ceased to exist so I am glad that I chose to work at Sedgewicks! They were the premier producers of equestrian leather in Walsall - supplying most of the local saddlers with their leather. I was offered a job in the Finishing Department, where the oils are applied to the horse leathers and where the colour is put on by hand, or by spraying or dyeing. I've been doing that since October 1970. I knew there would be no chance of advancement at Sedgewicks but I accepted that because I still liked the job and I've never wanted to do anything other than work with leather. I am still happy there today and hope to remain so until my retirement in twelve months time.

At Holden's I enjoyed opportunities to use my initiative. If I had an idea they used to say, "Don't tell us - just go and do it and then show us!" Today I have less chance to do that - they have their own set way of doing things and I have more feeling of just being a cog in the wheel, but, of course I'm only a mere youngster at Sedgewicks as I've only been there twenty years: the seventy year-old foreman has been there all his life. But we have the satisfaction of producing the best saddle leather in Walsall.

Leather-workers are a good crowd of people to work with, although there are less people around today who have their heart and soul in it. Many leather factories were small family businesses and some employers had a caring attitude as well as a desire to make money. We curriers were the boyos - we were close people who had usually worked together all our lives - and of course we played tricks on one another. For example every currier used to have his oil bucket, in which he also carried his wad - a soft squelchy slimy piece of mutton cloth with which to work the leather. At Holden's the premises were rat infested. They were real beauties - as big as a small cat. One day a rat was caught, beheaded, de-legged and de-tailed and dropped in Fred's bucket. He used to drink quite heavily on the Night Shift, and in his rather dazed state he would get the rat out and use it - until, eventually, he "smelled a rat"!

This is why working with leather is so satisfying. With leather there is no hard and fast rule - you can't work to a textbook. Leather is a material that was once alive and running about - it's not like a piece of metal that can be worked by machines. If you have five pieces of leather and put them through identical processes you will still get five different results. Working with leather is a challenge, even with the mechanised aids that have now been introduced. The twenty percent of the work that has to be done by hand can never be done by machine - it's work best done by the human eye, human hand and human brain striving to produce the perfect piece of leather. It's never boring or repetitive.

Jack Halksworth carries on working in his "retirement" giving demonstrations at the Walsall Leather Centre, photographed here in May 1989. (Photo: Anita Mehtra)

Jack Halksworth has brought many of his own templates with him to the Leather Centre, and in this workshop produces a variety of purses, handbags, wallets etc., Note the traditional gluepot on the burner. (Photo: Anita Mehtra)

Light Leather Goods

Jack Halksworth

My parents were not in the leather trade but I did have an ancestor who was. My ancestors came from the village of Eyam, the Plague Village, and only one Halksworth escaped the plague. I am descended from that person, and he was the local saddler.

I won a scholarship to the Walsall School of Art and Crafts as it was called in those days, to become a full time student. Everyone at that place had a choice of whatever career they wished to pursue after leaving and I had already made up my mind - I wanted to be a leather goods designer.

The first place I went to from the School of Art was a tiny little place called Wilmot Bennett's, in Midland Road, Walsall. They probably employed about fifty people, but in those days a lot of the factories were much larger, for example Mark Cross had hundreds of employees. The first thing that every youngster has to do is sweep up, and I had to do all the odd jobs like tea-making and running errands. You had to be "bound", or serve an apprenticeship for seven years. Later this decreased to five years. I was sixteen and a half when I started so I should have served a apprenticeship until I was twenty three, but I had my own ideas about that!

I didn't want to be "bound", and I eventually made up my mind to leave that place and go in search for another. I went to a little place in Little Newport Street. It was a German firm, almost entirely run by Germans and their ideas about the leather trade were

slightly different - in some respects better, in some respects not so good. That was in 1938 so I was only there a year when War broke out. The Germans immediately disappeared. On Monday 4th September I went down to the leather factory and it was all shut up. Most, but not all, the Germans were interned - so I was out of a job.

I went to John More and Co. in Wolverhampton Street, they produced an enormous range of leather goods and I realised that it was just the right place for me. I stopped there about two years, until I joined the RAF. I was then away from the trade for four or five years, but returned unscathed to John More's as an improver. From that I progressed to foreman, and I was a foreman for twenty two years.

I had the opportunity to learn many different aspects of making light leather goods, including handbags, purses, notecases, wallets, stud boxes, jewel boxes, and anything up to the size of a suitcase. The firm did make bridlery but that was an entirely separate section. Apart from that I did go round most of the different aspects of the leather trade that were carried out there, cutting, stitching, assembling light leather goods, costing, management, the lot!

I was hoping eventually to get the manager's job when it became vacant, but that didn't happen. The employer insisted that I was more useful to him on the practical side in pattern cutting and designing, where I was difficult to replace. It was easier for him to get someone else to be manager. So I realised that it would be difficult for me to advance in that firm - but I knew that I wanted to reach the top, I had no qualms about that!

At that time the Education Authorities in Walsall were asking for one or two experienced leather workers to become lecturers. I had all the qualifications for the job, such as UEI and RSA certificates, but what I was not prepared to teach was pure design - which is what they wanted me to teach. I wanted to teach industrial design, which is totally different. The so-called designer in any fashion business often designs things that just can't be made with the machinery available. To be an industrial designer you have to know what the machines can do. We could not agree on this, but as the years have gone by, it has become more apparent to everyone that the accent has to be on industrial design if we are to compete in foreign markets. We developed courses for the TOPS students (The Training Opportunities Scheme), the YOPS (The Youth Opportunities Scheme), and then the one and then the two year YTS schemes (Youth Training Scheme). For the last fifteen years I have been teaching industrial design and teaching the leather trade as it is today - both the old fashioned methods, and the most modern methods, until I retired last year. Since then I have been asked to give demonstrations in the Leather Centre.

The satisfaction of working in leather is that it has once been a living tissue. Every skin is different and working in leather is a handicraft. Plastic can replace leather in making some items but it can never replace it completely. It is very satisfying to turn out something that is both very nice to touch, but is also well designed. But you've got to live in this world and you do want rewards. My reward now is passing on my information to those entering the trade. It has always been enjoyable to work in the leather trade - but the pay was not good. The ordinary leather worker today is better paid than he used to be, but it is still not on a par with the financial reward enjoyed by people in mass production in other trades. We had a trade union but it was so small that it had to join up with a bigger union to survive, and it just seemed to be one of those trades where you could not command a high wage.

As leather workers we always had a good time. A nice crowd of people entered the trade and we got on well together. A lot of singing used to go on throughout the shop, but it was strict and you had to work hard to make your money - usually earning it on a piecework basis. It was impossible to learn everything even in ten lifetimes so you had to set out to master one section, in my case the light leather goods, but the trade is very sectionalised, and very specialised within the sections.

Straight Seams and Round Tops

Freda Shaw

When my friend and I left school together at the age of fourteen in 1925, we both wanted to work in the tailoring trade. We were very disappointed to find that there were no vacances at Shannons or Stammers, but we decided to see if we could find a job in the glove-making trade. At the firm of D.H.Powers they told us that they had some vacances and that they would set us on, for seven and sixpence a week. We thought that sounded grand.

The company had several different kinds of machinist. I was a prickseam-maker and had to learn to use the PXM machine, but there were also piki seams and round seams. We started our training by cutting out little palms, they gave us the fourchettes and we had to make the little quirkes. We had to make our seams very straight and produce neat round tops to the fingers. They were very strict and very particular about this, nevertheless they were a happy firm to work for. We had to learn to put the thumbs in and do side gussets if the gloves required them. It took about six months to learn the trade and be good enough at doing it. Then they let you start on a real pair of gloves and you really had to be careful! When we had made a dozen pairs of gloves we were paid our seven and sixpence (37p).

Eventually we went on to piecework. If you produced an extra ten shillings worth of gloves, the firm took half, and the other half was added onto your seven and sixpence. How proud we were of what we could earn! Sixpence was always deducted, however, for our white overalls. When I started at Power's all the rooms were full and the trainees had to learn the work in a small corner section of the room. I had to concentrate on what I was doing but once I had mastered glove-making I joined the big section and could join in singing all the old songs with the other girls. They didn't like us singing but could not really stop us. It seemed very cheerful as we sang and a room full of machines rattled away. We had a foremissis called Florrie Madeley who was killed in an accident and that was the saddest day that ever was at Power's.

The men at the factory always did the cutting out and stretching the leather - producing the back and

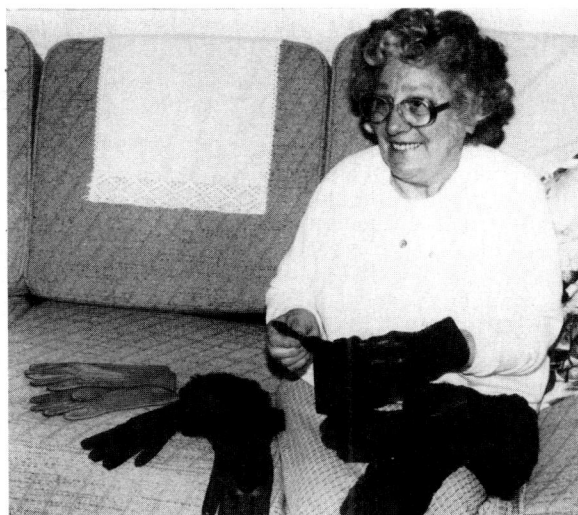

Freda Shaw displays her collection of leather gloves lovingly made over forty years ago for D.H. Powers of Walsall. Photographs of Freda at work can be seen in Alton Douglas's "Memories of Walsall", being published at the same time as this book. (Photo: Ned Williams)

front in one piece and the fourchettes. They brought them to us a dozen at a time. As time went on we could make four dozen pairs a week - earning about thirty shillings. As a machinist I was not allowed to leave my place. If I ran out of cotton I had to call Tillie, the errand girl. "Fetch some cotton, Tillie!" If you wanted a new needle someone had to fetch one for you. Mr.Arnold, the mechanic, came round and put the machine right if anything was going wrong. When I started there were eight of us to a table and ten tables of prickseam-makers, but later these numbers decreased.

We started at eight and finished at six but if there was plenty of work on we would only manage to get the actual machining done during the day. We would have to take the gloves home to finish the trimming and check the seams. Many times I sat up until eleven o'clock trimming the gloves. Next morning we took them back to work to "close them up" and trim them again - to make the perfect glove. We used to put them on our knees to press them out. Another department put the linings in if required and there was also a section that put fur on the gloves if that was wanted, and there was the topping department where they were finished off. When everything else had been done the gloves were pressed in Lottie Wood's department. They used to look beautiful by then if all the seams were perfectly straight and the tops perfectly rounded. Before they left the factory they were inspected and stamped with your mark. My mark was "L1" - this identified the gloves I made. It was very important not to leave any mark on the leather and therefore we were not supposed to eat at our machines.

I was selected to demonstrate glove-making at an exhibition at the Walsall Town Hall. We supplied gloves to Mr. Garnett Horton - a gentlemen's outfitter in Park Street, and I assembled gloves on his stand at the exhibition. After that I was sent to London for a fortnight and I felt very proud of myself then. I demonstrated glove-making in one of the large stores. Their buyer met me when I arrived in London, took me to lunch and then took me to my lodgings. The landlady's daughter also worked in the shop and they showed me round London at the weekend. At the end of the fortnight the buyer took me out to lunch again and put on my train back to the Midlands. I also made trips to Huddersfield and Newcastle on Tyne.

When the prickseam glove-making went slack I learnt to make the pika glove but I never learnt the hand-sewing. It was the only job I ever had because I left after I got married during the Second World War. But as soon as the firm was busy they asked me if I would have a machine at home, so I did that. Later, when I had moved to Nuneaton for a time, they would still bring me a machine if they were busy and I would make gloves at home! Its strange to think they have closed now. I think part of the business may have gone to Whitehouse and Cox in Marsh Street.

I will always remember the happy atmosphere at Power's. We were all good friends and Mr. Cook the foreman, who was a grand old chap, kept us all in order. We had one or two factory outings which we greatly enjoyed. The other day I was very happy to be re-united with Tillie, the errand girl, we have met again at the over-sixties club! We can both remember how once the work was our life. We sang at our machines and were proud of what we earned and proud of what we made. We even made gloves for Royalty - I think I made some gloves for Princess Marina - some shocking pink leather gloves! If I had a glove machine today I'd love to have another try - I'm sure I could still produce those straight seams and round tops!

The Works Outing — sometimes the only aspect of work that people have preserved in a photograph! In this picture Freda poses in the centre of a snap taken on the D.H.Powers outing to Llangollen, about 1930. On her right is Gladys, and on her left the errand girl, Tillie.

Buying Your Own Cotton

Joyce Oliver

There were no problems getting a job when I left school. you just went into whatever you wanted to do. I left at Easter in 1947, and the majority of work then for girls, other than office work, was in the tailoring, as well as in the leather trade. If you wanted a job you just went for an interview with the personel manager and you started on the following Monday.

I wanted to be a machinist in the trouser room but at first you had to stand up and do all the "trimming off", standing near the foreman's bench. We had to trim all the cotton ends off the finished garments to leave them clean. We did that for about the first month or six weeks, and then progressed to one of the machines as an apprentice. You were put next to one of the older ladies, and you had to do that for about nine months. After about a year I had become a machinist and then I was paid on piecework. Up until then I'd worked a forty eight hour week for twenty three and ninepence. (£1.19). We worked from eight in the morning until six at night - and longer on Friday - till a quarter past six, because the Wages Office didn't have the wages ready until then.

I assembled complete trousers, apart from the turn-ups. The button holes had to be done and the buttons sewn on. It fascinated me when I first went there to see buttons sewn on by a machine. The cutting was done in the room upstairs and all the cutters were men in those days. We made a lot of "made-to-measure" clothes so they all had to be made individually, cut out with big shears, whereas today they do layers and layers together with a cutting machine. The tailoring used to create a lot of dust.

The sewing machines were belt-powered Jones' machines and although they had mechanics to look after them I never had to have a mechanic to a machine once - they were that good. The sewing room was very long, like a large hall. At one end they made coats, and at the bottom end they made waistcoats. We were the trouser section. We used to have a lady on the big Hoffman steam presses with the big iron, and when you'd done a certain ammount of trousers you had to bundle them up and pass them to her. She had to press all the seams out and you fetched them back when they were pressed to finish them off. I never had the opportunity to swap around - I just made trousers. There were men tailors, however, who made complete suits. You could never really earn a lot because the price of the work was so low. We earned 1/9 (9p) for completing a trouser right through - white calico pockets and all, and no zips like modern trousers!

The building used to remind me of a barracks block or a prison - something like Dartmoor! The stairs were all stone steps and the toilets, just off the workroom, were the old closet type - quite primitive really. There were some single ladies there that looked really old to us. They must have been there all their working lives. There was no union - they weren't allowed. If anyone tried to start a union they were sacked - automatically sacked. I worked in three sewing factories up until I was married and unions were not allowed in any of them.

Things were on coupons then, just after the War, and the colours of everything were very conservative

- not like today. And one amazing thing about that place was that you had to buy your own cotton! You had to go to the lady who marked your work off: Little Aggy. She sat behind a high desk and you went there to have your work booked in. You had to order your cotton on the Friday for it to be ready for the Monday morning. If you ran out of cotton and had to buy one of the bigger spools of black, or white, or grey, it really set you back when it was taken out of your money. When I think about it now it seems utterly ludicrous that we bought the cotton for their work.

It was a proper Victorian place, but there is one positive thing I can say about it. Shannon's tailoring was "spot on". They did all Burton's tailoring from Walsall. Even until recently, until the factory was closed down, whenever I've gone into a menswear shop I've been able to pick out a Shannon's suit because of the quality and the finishing-off. Even to this day, when I go out with my husband for a suit I find myself picking all sorts of bits and pieces out and find myself saying, "No, that's not finished off nicely!"

After I had been there a year or two they started a social club that used to meet on Wednesday nights, and we had an annual dance in the Town Hall. We even started having a Shannon's Beauty Queen. But after three or four years there I left. I'd had enough.

The sewing room in Edgar Stammers' factory in Walsall in the 1930s. The foreman, Alfred Turley, stands in the centre to the left. Both at Stammers and Shannons there was a clear demarcation between men's work (cutting) and women's work (sewing). (Walsall Local History Centre)

Cutting the Cloth

Howard Freeman

I was born in 1908, and as a child I lived in New Street, very close to St. Matthew's Church, Walsall. I could see the clock from where I live. The houses aren't there any more. It was a busy area then but it seems so dead today.

When I first left school I was out of work but I did some part-time work for a hairdresser across the road, lathering his customers for him. One day a pal of mine came round to ask me to play football, and he worked at Stammers - the factory a few hundred yards from where I lived where they made clothes for Foster Brothers. Somehow I got a job at Stammers as well.

When I first started I was just pushing the truck about - taking the work from the cutting room to the sewing room in bundles. But later I had the chance to go to Night School to learn to be a cutter. Edgar Stammers was a very good boss and he was also a local councillor. On the council he sat on the Education Committee and he had a lot to do with setting up this Night School where we could go to learn our trade. We learnt how to draught a pattern from the customer's measurements, and how to cut it out.

At Stammers we cut everything - jackets, trousers, vests, overcoats. The patterns were made of card - called pattern paper, and we marked the cloth round the pattern with a piece of clay. The pattern was made to fit a normal sized person but the job would arrive with a ticket attached on which the shop which took the measurements would record any special features of the customer. For example the customer might have a long neck, or short one, or be stooped, hump-backed or corpulent. For example; it might say "SRB" meaning "Slightly Round Back". The cutters skill lay in cutting the cloth to take these thing into account.

The cutters were always men, but the garments were then taken to the trimmers and fitters, who were usually girls. They would select the right lining material and cut it out to fit before passing the garment onto the machinists. The sewing was done by machine, but we had a machine that could make it look hand sewn - "Hand-sewn by machine", we used to say! I eventually married one of the trimmers.

While making the patterns I was sometimes used as a model, because, at the time, I was a perfect size 36. They used me to try things on, to get them perfect, and then the same pattern could be used to be graded up to 38, 40 and 42. After 42 you needed to make a different pattern altogether.

We worked from eight thirty in the morning until six thirty at night with an hour and a quarter for lunch. Sometimes you could work till nine o' clock at night if we were busy. Saturdays we worked until dinnertime, and we would work on Sundays, at double time, if we were busy. We always had work to do but even if it was slack they kept us on. Once you were a passed-out skilled cutter I felt you earned a decent wage - say about three guineas a week top rate.

All the cutters knew each other, whether we worked at Stammers or Shannons, which was just across the way. In fact I played for Shannons football team. There are very few of us cutters left now, and the trade has practically died out. I was in the Tailor and Garment Workers Union and served on the committee for a time.

When the ⸺ came along my hereditary deafness prevented me going in the services but I had to go on War work. I built aeroplane wings. The wings were huge, and I had to go inside and push the bolts up through the wings so that the girl outside could put the bolt on. When the War finished I went to Shannons, but the work wasn't there. I suppose the chaps were still in the forces. There was a different way of doing things at Shannons - you had to be very careful at Shannons and stick very carefully to the pattern. you couldn't alter things like we did at Stammers.

Cutting was a complicated skill to learn but once you had mastered it,it was a piece of cake. The only problems you had were with exceptional measurements. I once had to make a suit for a man with a 72" seat and a 69" chest - fantastic measurements! The boss said, "We've got a right job here for you Chick!" Cutting it out involved a lot of guesswork and I was worried to death about it. We cut it out, basted it together, and sent it over to the shop in Wolverhampton for the customer to try it on.

They sent for me to see it on the customer, to see what needed doing to it. I had to go Wolverhampton and have a look at the chap. He was too large for my tape measure to go round. I had to re-mark it up and then re-cut it. We sent it back to the shop and heard no more about it. After two months I asked my boss what had become of it. "Oh - that was OK - it was a lovely fit. In fact he's coming back for another one!" My boss had never bothered to tell me, but then he wasn't really bothered as long as he got his money for it!

Betty Smith - The Dressmaker

Elizabeth Stead

I was born on 18th May 1899, the second child of Simeon and Alice Smith of Darlaston. I was born under the sign of Taurus and we are supposed to be very inventive people. I was certainly a very busy child, always wanting to do things constructively, and always knitting! Even before I went to school I was knitting black stockings for my sisters to wear to school, and I remember knitting a pair of garters with rainbow wool.

My mother and father were friendly with a woman who was a hat-maker but they did not think there would be a good living to made from doing that, so they took me to a Miss Fletcher and apprenticed me to the dressmaking. It was only an ordinary house and I had to work with two other apprentices in a pokey little room. There we was no electric light - just gas light and no electric sewing machine - just an ordinary treadle machine. I worked there for two years for no wages at all, simply because I was an apprentice.

I worked from eight thirty in the morning until eight o' clock at night. I had one hour off for lunch in which I had a two mile walk each way to and from where we lived in Darlaston. We had Thursday afternoon off but on Saturday we worked unitl eight thirty. And all this was for no wages. If my father went for a drink and was merry when he came back he used to give me a threepenny bit, and ... was all the money I had.

Folks knew I could do sewing so they asked me to do it for them. I put a band on skirt for a woman and charged her fourpence - but she didn't pay me because she felt that I shouldn't charge her! That was during the First World War, and I had a friend who was getting married at that time. I made her wedding dress in navy blue whipchord trimmed with pretty flowered silk on the boddice - and that was after I'd been dressmaking for only twelve months.

I carried on, getting up at six in the morning and doing a bit of sewing before going to work until eight at night. My mother was very kind and did everything she possibly could to help. My life was so filled with work that I never went to see a film. Cinema films were just beginning at that time but I never had time to see one! My only recreation was singing, which I really enjoyed. I sang in the choir at the Methodist Chapel and later joined Darlaston Choral Society. The Methodist chapels used to have anniversaries and I had to sew all the dresses for the girls on the platform to wear. I was sewing fourteen hours a day!

After my two year apprenticeship, I became an Improver and earned three and sixpence a week (17½p). I was mainly making costumes - skirts and little jackets, all lined of course. But after three months I left and started working on my own from home.

I acquired lots of customers very quickly, and I was called, "Betty Smith, the Dressmaker". If people had a dressmaker in those days they considered themselves very fortunate because ready made clothes were not very good then. In fact they were shoddy. Some people were very particular and fussy about the quality of the work, others didn't know what they wanted. Some would say, "Make me one like the one you've got." But I was always very wary of that and didn't like anyone having one like mine!

When I got married I made the dresses. I had two sisters, one was in rose pink and the other was in blue and all round the bottom I worked ribbon on it. Those dresses stole the show, because they were so out of the ordinary. Several people asked me to make dresses like them but I wouldn't.

Thus I spent my life sewing. Then, when I was fifty I decided to give it up. I went to work - I got a job in a factory making cookers. I used to test the thermostats, until the factory closed. My father-in-law had seen an advert for repairers at the Supreme Laundry in Wednesbury so I went to work for them. I repaired shirts and sheets, using a machine, but it was murder because it was so hot in the department where I worked. I stayed three years.

In the meantime Sketchley's wanted a repairer at Darlaston so I went there. I did me good - I really learnt a lot. And I've saved many a man's reputation by putting a new zip in his trousers. At the time people were having their trousers tapered and their dresses shortened, so those were other jobs I learnt to do. I learnt so much because it taught me how ready-made clothes were made and it gave me a lot of ideas. I stayed there six years.

Later my life changed completely and I went to South Africa for four years when Rubery Owen sent my son-in-law over there, but I still carried on making clothes for my grandaughters. Even now I continue

to enjoy making things. I have really devoted my life to sewing. A real seamstress has no time for other things - like housework! Of course I had to do it, but sometimes in the middle of doing a room all of a sudden I'd think, "I'll just get on with that thing I'm making." ....and I'd just sit down in the middle of the room and get on with the sewing.

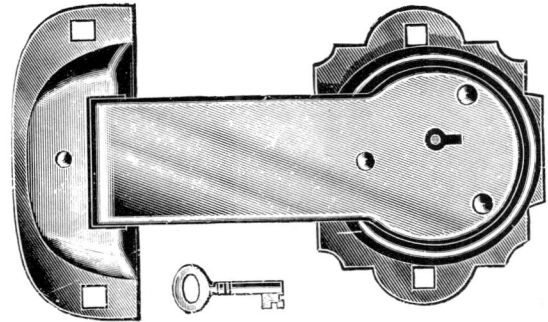

To Master and Differ

Tom Millington

From the age of five to the age of fourteen I went to the Lane Head Board Schools. Two years before I left school, at the age of twelve, I went into a lock factory doing odd jobs and gaining experience of the trade. I worked from 4 o'clock when I came out of school till 8 o'clock, and often worked on Saturdays and Sundays as there was so much work about - but the pay was not too good.

At first there were only about four other workers in this small workshop and Frank Dunscombe was the gaffer, but by the time I had left school and gone to work for him fulltime he had built a new plant beside the original workshop. It was next door to where I lived so going to work was very easy - just a matter of going next door! As a full time worker I did forty seven hours for 6/- a week (30p)

I didn't do an apprenticeship - it was just a matter of doing an ordinary week's work, but by the age of fourteen I was already experienced because I had started young - and really I think it's better that way. The boss came to me and said, "Here you are, Tom - here's your first order to make locks on your own." And I made a gross of locks on my own.

When you get to know a bit about the trade you find it is very interesting. In the cabinet and furniture lock trade you're never doing exactly the same work from week to week. The variety is possible because there are two or three hundred different types of lock that you can make. Wardrobes, cupboards, cabinets all require different locks. It is not like doing a job today - today's work is all repetition, which is boring. And today they only assemble the locks - not make 'em as we did in those days. When I first started we had no machinery whatsoever - everything had to be done by hand. The drilling and countersinking was done on a foot-worked treadle lathe, and that was the only machine we had.

First of all you have to learn how to file, and you have to learn what kind of file to use for each job. In

A Locksmiths' shop using belt driven machinery to assist in the manufacture of cabinet locks at Richard Cooper & Son's works in Wolverhampton around the time of the First World War. (authors collection)

files there are variations - a file can be rough, in between or smooth, and to do the finishing you get what we call a buff stick - a piece of wood about fourteen inches long, and you put a piece of emery cloth on and finish your work off.

In the new factory we did have machines to do some of the jobs we had previously done by hand, for example we had a linnisher, a machine with a revolving emery belt which replaced some of the filing, and we also had drillers - just pull a handle down instead of pedalling with your foot. At first the machines were belt-driven but they were eventually motorised. In those days I had long hair, and once, as I was doing some drilling I bent my head down and my hair caught in the spindle and pulled my head right up to the driller - and pulled my hair out!

I stayed there until I was 19. Then me and a girl in the stores had an argument. In those days when you had a new file it was recorded in a book, and you were supposed to make it last a month. My file was wore out, although I hadn't had it a month. I said to the girl, "This one's hopeless, I cor work with this." She says, "Yo' cor 'ave one - your time's not up." I caught hold of her wrist and bruised it. She showed the bruise to the gaffer and I got the sack.

I left and got another job at Henry Squire's of New Invention. When I went to be interviewed he said, "What can you do in the lock trade?"

I said, "Roughly everything. I've had a good training so I can make any type of cabinet lock."
He says, "Can you differ and master?"
"Yes I can."
He says, "If you can do that, then you've been a poor paid man. So, I'll tell you what I'll do, Tom, I'll put you on a month's trial and I'll give you £3 a week to start. At the end of the month if we find you satisfactory and you have shown you can do what you say you can do, we will rise it accordingly."

I had only been earning £2 a week, so I was pleased. "Differ and master" is where you make a lock that will pass only its own key and yet will pass a master key that can also pass all the different locks.

So on went the month. We had our money in cans in those days and when the month came to an end I went along on Friday night to pick up my can and I found there was £4 in it. I went up to the office and asked if they had made a mistake. "Oh no," they said. "the boss said he would rise you accordingly, and he has done."

I stayed there until I went to work one morning and, to our astonishment, the place had burned down - and we were all out of work. I had to go down and sign on the Labour, which was a thing I didn't much care for, but, at the time, my brother was going round the streets selling fruit and potatoes. He bought me a horse and cart and I started doing the same until I

56

got my job back in the locks. My brother used to hawk Willenhall and I used to hawk Bloxwich, and when I returned to the locks Joe took over both the rounds and built the business up. I had enjoyed it until the winter came with the frosts. On certain roads I had to hold the horse up - had to get off the cart and lead him.

About the same time I went to the World Scout Jamboree at Birkenhead - attended by 52000 scouts from 52 countries. I had been in the scouts since I was ten and went as patrol leader of the 1st. Willenhall Troop. After I got married in 1933 I still went on with my scouting - then I took on another job - a shop steward in the lock trade.

I had not been a person to stay in one place - cos I could never stand to be out of work and as soon as the work became short in a place they would find I'd gone! I'd hear "talk", and I'd be gone. In all I worked in eighteen different places. One day, during the Second World War. the boss came to me and said, "Tom, I want you to go down to the Union and get them to come up here and get the Union organised here." So I did that, and at the meeting we held I was elected as Shop Steward.

It may seem strange for a boss to ask for the Union to be formed at his place, but the thing was the Union had done him a favour and he thought that maybe there was some good in this Union business - so he might as well have one in his works - Harold Smith's of Wolverhampton. During the War it was difficult to move round as everything was directed by the Ministry of Labour. Mr.Smith had wanted me to work for him and the Union had helped fix this with the Manpower Board - and he seemed to enjoy that.

I was with the Union - the Lock & Metal Workers, for twentyfive years, wherever I worked, and my life was always busy with the Union and the Scouts and the Locks. Even at the last place I worked - Fox and Morgan - I was the shop steward. It was a fairly big place, about sixty people worked there and we didn't have much trouble with the gaffer although he was the sort of fellow who would cut down on labour if he thought there was an opportunity to do so. But one dispute did lead to quite an argument.

We had an Indian girl working in the bobbin shop. In the bobbin shop the men were on top rate, and also had a bonus for doing the work in dusty conditions. I asked the Indian girl one day what rate she was being paid and found that she was only getting what the girls got in the ordinary factory. I went to see the boss about it.

He said, "Tom, I'm not paying any girl above the rate."
I said, "You're doing wrong, and I'm asking you to pay the proper rate - you've got the book with all the rates in. I'm asking you to give that girl the bobbin rate - and I also want her to have the bonus that you are paying the men."
He said, "It's out, Tom."
I said, "Right, it's out. I'll go down the Union and bring them up here," which is what I did do. We talked it over and he eventually rose her rate and gave her the bonus. After this success one or two other folks joined the Union! - the types who used to say, "Why should I pay, if I haven't go to?"

The chaps and the girls in the lock trade never had much to do with fixing wages as it was always settled between the Union and an employers' organisation. Relations were generally good but we had some tough times. the Union has only ever had two strikes - once in 1926, the General Strike, and another one about ten years ago with a certain local firm.

The most interesting thing has always been making locks. I didn't really want to retire before seventy but my wife was ill so I left at 65. I am 79 now and have been at the Willenhall Lock Museum since it started. It gives me a chance to talk to people about locks, and really I don't think the people in the trade understand it. They just work there and forget the trade in general - they just assemble the mass-produced components without really understanding locks. When you get to the bottom of it - when you understand them, its really marvellous.

I give them a straight covered lock, which you could put in a wardrobe, a double 'un - one where the bolt can shoot out either side. I tell them its a four lever lock, and ask them how many differs do they think I could make on that lock, where the key would not pass any other lock? The answer is 20,736! But the trouble is, even if I simply ask them, "Can you differ?" - they don't know what I'm talking about. I don't agree with automation because it puts people out of work, but it's also sad if the trade has changed so much that people don't understand locks.

Tom Millington demonstrates the art of filing at the Willenhall Lock Museum in May 1989, surrounded by files and lock components. On his apron he wears the badge of the Lock & Metal Workers Union. (Photo: Sarah Wood)

A Family Business

Harold Fletcher

This business goes back to my Grandfather's time. His name, Henry Edward Fletcher, is still the name under which we trade today, and we are still on the same premises. The business passed to the brothers and sisters of my father's generation, and they carried it on for a long time. As a child I came and watched the others working which was natural as we lived and worked on the same premises.

When I left school in 1934 I think it was expected that I would automatically join the family business. I didn't think about it much - I just started work in this workshop when I was fourteen and began doing simple things. I sorted out keys and castings, ran errands, and did a little filing. We had a massive hand press for blanking out components, and it took two men to operate it. One stood and pulled the sway round, the other helping with a rope. That was one of the first jobs I did.

When I started we had just had electricity installed. Up until then our power came from a gas engine out at the back, with its own massive water tank. It was very powerful and could drive our first power press, and drove everything via shafts, pulleys and belts. After the electricity came, each of the machines was motorised.

Learning the trade was a gradual process and you had to wait for a year or two before you were allowed to make a lock. The older people made the locks and I had to prepare the parts for them. By learning little jobs and watching the others work I progressed slowly, but I think it was faster in a family business than going through a long apprenticeship in a big factory. I had the chance to learn such a variety of jobs - filing, pressing, lathe work, drilling, and all manner of jobs.

We solely make cabinet locks - to be used on cupboards, drawers, boxes etc. and the production in this factory has stayed the same over the years. We are still making just the same locks, but we are making more than we used to, because the tools and equipment have been modernised. The previous generations did so much work by hand but we have had to modernise in order to remain competitive. What we have done is change some of the techniques of maunufacture. Whereas they used to stand at the vice and knock in drill pins and stumps, this job is now done on the hand press, which is three times quicker. We can also use the power press for doing several things in one operation. We have one or two old fashioned ways which can't be altered when it comes to our type of locks.

One or two of our customers have been taking our locks for seventy five years, but many others have gone out of business. Even fifty years ago your customers were your friends - there was a bond between us, but that personal friendship in business seems to have gone today. Of course, there are not many ironmongers today and that is where most of our work went, or to wholesale factors. We still supply cabinet lock wholesalers, and they supply the furniture manufacturers and carpenters.

My brother, Mervyn, started in 1950, and the pair of us actually took over the business in August 1962. Now there is just the two of us and our wives working here. Women have always worked here - doing the pressing jobs and the lighter work. Occasionally women have worked on the bench, knocking stumps in and rivetting them over onto the case of the lock. The stump is the part of the lock where the lever or tumbler fits on. The drill pin is the part of the lock where the key is drilled and passes down over it.

The real craftsmanship comes at the bench - the different throws of the levers, and cutting the keys to them - you have to learn that by doing lots and lots of it. Some locks are all the same; it becomes a habit making one after another, but it is more interesting when you have to make different ones. The fathers and uncles used to pass little tips about making individual locks - for example, if there is a lttle bit of fray on the spring it helps the spring to stop in the tumbler.There are various little tricks like that which can be passed on from father to son.

Just because we are sitting here by the same stove that has heated this workshop since I was a lad you must not think that things have not changed. We have motorised the machines, modified the tooling and simplified the manufacturing processes. Today less people produce more locks and we even pack them

Left: Harold & Mervyn Fletcher at the door of their cabinet lock factory – a typical Black Country industrial building. (Ned Williams) *Right: Harold watches Marjorie Fletcher working on the hand press.* (Anita Mehtra) *Both pictures taken in June 1989.*

in boxes of tens although we still like to call a gross a gross! The problem is that you don't see locks on furniture today. In the old houses every drawer, cupboard and wardrobe had a lock and the door of the house was probably left open! Today it is reversed - the furniture has no locks but the doors and windows of the house are treated to a major security operation!

I suppose we have enjoyed a life of lock-making but its been hard work even with our modernisation. I would say that, in the past, lock-making has been one of the lowest paid industries, and that is why many others have left it over the years. And yet we decided to come into it and have stayed in it. Perhaps there is just a satisfaction in working for yourself. Receiving an order and working on it from start to finish - that is what gives you satisfaction at the end of the day. We are the last of the line: when we finish - that's it.

Motorcycle Madness

Albert Clarke

My life seems inextricably linked with the cycle and motor cycle trades that once flourished in Wolverhampton - a world that has now vanished completely. One of the intriguing figures from that world was Howard Davies. He made TT racing history in 1921 by coming second in the Junior Race and then used the same Wolverhampton-built AJS machine to win the Senior Race!

I first met Howard Davies when I was eight, in 1910. He was a friend of my family and my Uncle Jack got him his first job with AJS. He was about two years older than me. More significant was the occasion when he approached me in the middle of 1924, when we were both young men in our twenties. He told me he was manufacturing motor bikes and he had booked a stand at the forthcoming Motor Show at Olympia. Would I give him a hand in getting ready for the show?

We went over to a little factory in East Street, Heath Town. It was an old cycle factory that had closed. Inside I found almost nothing - just a few lugs and bits of frames and an artist's impression of what HRD's motor bikes were going to look like. The artist, Massey, had certainly produced a sleek good looking bike, but no one had any idea how it was going to be made - and the Motor Show was only a week away! Somehow we accomplished a miracle. We worked non-stop for seventy five hours and produced four HRD bikes in that week. It was impossible - but we did it. When the hall was closing at Olympia on the Saturday night - with our stand still empty - I was still chasing round Wolverhampton getting parts of the bikes plated - and getting platers out of the pub to do it. In the early hours of Sunday morning we set off for London in a van. We had to bribe the Night Watchman at Olympia to let us in and give us access to the empty stand. On Monday morning, as the show opened, the stand proudly displayed the four HRD machines.

We gained enough orders to really launch the HRD motorcycle, but, to my horror, Howard decided to start making TT bikes instead of production models. All my talent was used in getting these racers built and this paid off in 1925 when Howard came second in the Junior, and then won the Senior.It was another miracle. There were only four or five of us working at the East Street works, and I was the only one who knew enough to be able read a micrometer. I acted as manager for HRD from about 1926 to 1927 but the orders had dried up. The General Strike seemed to kill off the trade, and in that period when nobody seemed to be buying motorbikes I gave up the trade, except to help a couple of amateur racers such as Jim Potts.

To try and understand how I came to be involved with motorcycles at all it is necessary to understand my family history. My grandfather was John Pickard. When he died in 1922 he was Wolverhampton's oldest resident. He was reckoned to be 104. He had been a blacksmith and he came to Wolverhampton in that capacity to work for the Shrewsbury and Birmingham Railway as they established their works at Stafford Road. In turn all that became part of the GWR and John Pickard worked fifty years for the railway. If you wanted anything made in wrought iron - he could make it. My father built a small workshop for him,

Albert Clarke, and his late wife Anne, pose with the 1901 Wearwell motorised cycle built by his father's company. Photographed in 1986 by Rob Taylor for the Black Country Bugle.

where he had his anvil, blocks, clamps and whetstone. My grandfather taught me, as a child, how to harden and temper, and all the tricks of tempering. For example to quench material when it was blood red it had to be dipped into moving water in the bosh. If the water was not in motion it would itself be heated rather than quench the iron. I also learned how to use the whetstone - I had to turn it while he used it.

My other grandfather, who died before I was born, was Henry Clarke, a wheelwright. He had married Harriet Powney, whom I remember well from my childhood. She came from a family of Wombourne nailers. Henry founded the Cogent Cycle Company in 1868. My father, William Clarke, helped start the Wearwell Cycle Works in Darlington Street, one of the town's most successful cycle manufacturers. They also built motor cycles but my father regarded cycles as his "bread and butter". He assured me that people would still be riding pedal cycles long after motorcycles had come and gone

As a child I rode a motorcycle round the gravel paths at home and learnt to strip and build an engine, as well as learning the secrets of my grandfather's trade. I started my first "job" at ten, because my father allowed me to spend my school holidays at the works. The first job I was given to do was blackleading the joints of a frame. A kid had to put black lead round the joint, using a stiff brush, wiping the parts where you didn't want the brass to run when the frame was brazed.

My next job was "pegging". They used to knock the tubes in, after dipping them in wet borax, and I used to peg them with a small bench drill and knock the pegs in. Finally I was allowed to do the brazing, but

The HRD workshops established in the Isle of Man for the 1925 TT races. Albert Clarke is in the top left background of the picture, partly obscured by the handlebars of bike no. 1.
(Albert Clarke's collection)

the filers didn't like it as I put the brass on too thickly. I learnt everything by asking the old sweats what they knew, and although I didn't go to college or anything like that, I taught myself to use the engineering measuring instruments. Most of the time rule of thumb prevailed and trial an error was the basic working method. I learnt to do most things except building wheels quickly. Building and trueing a wheel is an art.

As I left school the First World War came along and I enlisted at sixteen and a half. I served as an aeroplane fitter in the R.F.C. When I came out of the services, my father was trying to re-constitute the cycle and motorcycle business. I worked in the machine shop and helped assemble a variety of machines for Wulfruna, for Ortbit, in Sedgely Street, and made the frames for the Olympic. Generally I was getting fed up with the motorcycle trade as the slump came along in 1923. I started my own business dealing in Government Surplus materials, and then came 1924 and Howard Davies' call for assistance!

After leaving HRD in 1927 I was able to return to building up my own business. We manufactured garage equipment such as cylinder head grinders and valve re-facers. I remained in this business until 1975.

Born to be an Engineer

Geoff Stevens

I don't know if one is born an engineer, or even how one becomes an engineer, but I was born in 1913 into an engineering family and grew up expecting to go into the family business. As a child I played with Meccano and if I was given a new toy I could take it to pieces - and put it all together again but I don't know whether that had anything to do with it. It may have had something to do with the time that I grew up in. I sometimes think I have had the best possible seventy six years through which to have lived. I remember seeing my first aeroplane and airship - we were called

out into the garden to see them. We not only saw them but we could understand how they worked. When radio came along I could build a crystal set with cardboard and bits of wire. Today if you want to put a video on its as much as you can cope with to know how to load the machine and which button to press - we haven't a clue how it works! If you open a calculator there is nothing to see, but all the things I grew up with were capable of being appreciated and understood.

When I was old enough to have a motorbike I was given one, because fortunately my father could afford to do that. I promptly took it to pieces, put it together again and knew exactly how it worked. And then I went out on it just for the joy of riding it. We didn't ride motorbikes to get to work or to go from A to B, we rode just for the pleasure of doing it, and we felt the same about cars. Today machines are functional - not a source of pleasure in themselves. My father and my Uncles and Aunts were all motor cycle enthusiasts and had built up the Wolverhampton firm of AJS from nothing.

My grandfather, Joe Stevens Snr., born way back in the 1850s, had been a blacksmith in Wednesfield. He had five sons and four daughters. His son Harry built had started making engines in Grandfather's workshop. He had acquired his skills helping his father make press tools and special purpose machines to sell to the lock trade. All five brothers were very good engineers. They could do machine work, design and make machine tools and had a flair for design. They were also good business men. The AJS was often compared with Sunbeam in the motor cycle world, and with Star and Clyno in the car world but the Stevens brothers did not have the flying start that John Marston, Wolverhampton's great benefactor, had at Sunbeam. As an engineer he was a perfectionist and was wealthy enough to employ the best managers and best designers to build Sunbeam cars and motorcycles. I believe he never rode a motorbike, and possibly never drove a car. On the other hand, my family, including my aunts, were all enthusiasts.

The first production AJS bikes rode out of the Retreat Street works before I was born and I was only a baby when the work was moved to new premises at Graisley Hill. I joined the firm in 1929, when I was sixteen, and was fortunate to see the company at the peak of its productivity. The trade suffered terrible seasonal fluctuations but about that time the company was capable of producing six hundred motorcycles in a week. That was the size of the business they had created, although, ironically its end was not far off.

When I started I was put in the toolroom and began to learn my trade from scratch. I had not been there very long before I was sent for a brief spell in the Sales Department. I did not understand why at the time but it became clearer to me later. My father realised the firm would go into liquidation and thought the sales experience would be useful to me. At least in the short time I worked at AJS I had the chance to experience the very happy atmosphere that existed there. I never got involved in racing. I went to trials but did not ride in them, but at the works the racing and trials riders were just people who worked in the factory. George Rowley, one of our top trials riders was the machine shop foreman's son, and Leo Davenport, who once won the TT, was the Works Manager's son. If someone came along to take their photograph they were sent home to put their plus fours on, and afterwards went back into the factory to get on with their work.

When AJS went into liquidation we sold the goodwill to Colliers, manufacturers of the Matchless motorcycles and we discovered the immense loyalty that everyone felt towards the firm. One fellow was asked by Colliers to come back into the factory and help pack up jigs and fixtures for despatch to their factory in London. That man came round to my father and asked him if he would mind him taking a job with Matchless - or would it be disloyal? My father told him that if he was offered a job he would be wise to take it. George Rowley felt very "guilty" about going to Matchless and we had to beg him to realise the the AJS was closed. He was a free man - he could go where he liked. Later I discovered the atmosphere and relationships in other firms could be very different.

Although the firm had to go into liquidation, we were not bankrupt, and all the creditors were paid in full. When AJS (1914) ltd., had moved to Graisley the brothers had made over the Retreat Street works to their sisters and father as the Stevens Screw Company. After the liquidation they went to their father and asked if they could have the Retreat Street Works back. They moved back there and drew up plans to start making a Stevens three-wheeler van. This was to be a cheap commercial vehicle costing about £70 at a time when the smallest Austin or Morris van would cost just over £100.

The vehicle was designed by Harry Stevens, and was fitted with a 600cc water-cooled engine. It had one wheel at the front and two at the back.. If the front wheel was locked right over to ninety degrees the whole thing would rotate in its own length! This had to be prevented on production models because errand boys would lock the wheel over, rev up the engine, let in the clutch and drive forward until they broke the front fork!

In making this vehicle I did machining, turning flywheels and machining cylinder heads. As well as lathe work I worked on jigs that Harry Stevens had designed for drilling the main frame. I did other drilling jobs on the forks, brakes and anchor plates. In the early days we worked on batches of six at a time. We made sufficient parts for six. Six three wheelers were then laid down in a row and then we went back to square one and made another six. It involved no more than about a dozen of us, and it was quite an achievement to turn out six well made vehicles at a time in such a small works. I was still really very much a trainee as I was still under 21.

I worked at Retreat Street long enough to see the first three wheeler reach the road but then I left and I don't think I ever went in the works again. From this distance of time I think one of most interesting points about my experience there is that it has enabled me to verify that we did make the engines there. We didn't buy them in - We didn't even buy the frames, we made those ourselves, but we did buy in standard parts like tyres and mudguards.

AJS moto cycles rolling off the production line at the end of the 1920's when the company was capable of producing up to 600 motor cycles a week. (Geoff Stevens' collection)

When I left the company I went to work for John Roper, a very well known engineer in a small works in Upper Villers Street. During my time there I gained much useful experience. I was machining on centre lathes and turret lathes, but I didn't do any gear cutting as the Ropers kept that in the family. It was production work - making cut-price spares for motor cars. They were precision items like crown wheels and pinions, and gears, in batches of twenties and fifties.

Then I went over to Longbridge, to the Austin. It was a very nasty shock! I had been warned about Brummies and I took it all with a pinch of salt, but it was true. They wouldn't help a newcomer at all, and the only people who spoke to me socially during the first few weeks were from Wolverhampton! Perhaps everything was different in an organisation like the Austin just by virtue of its size. I remember that there were no chucks on the drills - you had to have your own chuck in your own tool kit and guard it like a hawk. At Ropers if you had left a sixpence on the bench no-one would have touched it! The other sad thing is that travelling to and from Longbridge every day from Wolverhampton left me no time to keep in touch with what Stevens were doing and I did not see the new Stevens motorbike being built that was introduced in 1934.

I got used to the Austin and worked elsewhere as an engineer but I never came across the same atmosphere and friendliness and enthusiasm that I had known in Wolverhampton. Although the four manufacturers were rivals they were also friends who got on well together. We used to do work for Clyno, and, of course, AJS and Sunbeam were next door to one another so the testers used to go out together and would often have "off the record" discussions about what each firm was doing. The first Sunbeam engine that they built themselves was designed by Harry Stevens. Their engineer, John Greenwood, developed it, and his son, Cyril, was one of the people who worked at AJS until the end! Thats how close we all were. Even now if I run into old AJS folk they come up and speak about my father and my uncles, and now that I am retired I am trying to piece together their story that was never properly recorded at the time.

Lasting Contacts

Malcolm Palmer

I worked for Contactor Switchgear Ltd., Blakenhall, Wolverhampton, for thirty five years, in which time I saw a happy efficient family firm prosper and grow and then decline through a series of take-overs. As a loyal workforce we always believed that we would survive, that we would go on re-emerging from these take-overs like a phoenix rising from the ashes but in the end that was not the case.

Contactor Switchgear had started in 1936 when two men, Harry Rayner and Jeanne Liwski acquired a licence to maunfacture switchgear to the design of a French firm - La Telemecanique Electrique. Including the founders, the firm began with a workforce of eight, but they had a good product and the high cost of tooling and setting up production paid off. Work began in premises in Moorfield Road - a part of Wolverhampton associated with many famous industrial enterprises. The machine shop established in 1943 was once used by Sunbeam to build their 1920s record car. Many people who joined the firm as it progressed stayed for the rest of their working lives - it was that sort of place. One old chap I knew as a foreman in the Test Department had arrived in 1938 and he was a genius with electrical switchgear - he knew it outside in and inside out, and was treated like an adopted son by the founders. We prided ourselves that we built the "Rolls Royce" of switchgear, even though we never became as mighty as the giants like GEC and English Electric. Of course there had been another company in Wolverhampton in that field - the Electric Construction Company - and before the War they tried to prevent their employees leaving and coming to Contactor!

My first acquaintance with Contactor Switchgear was just after the War. It was before I had left school and I started travelling about with my Uncle in his coal lorry. About 1948/49 we used to call at Moorfield Road to collect scrap from Contactor. It was a fascinating place. There were the Sunbeam premises where they had been making trolley buses, later I saw Villiers motor bikes coming off the production line, and

Malcolm Palmer (on the right) and Jimmy Green in the spares "overload test" department at Contactor Switchgear in 1963. The photograph was taken by Mr. Vaughan, a director of the Australian branch of the firm.

I remember seeing lines of "Yeoman of England" tractors, made by Turner's, standing in Moorfield Road. Nowadays we would think of the area as an "industrial estate" and obviously it had been a prime German target during the War. Many old Contactor employees entertained me with their stories of fire-watching and the Home Guard.

I started work with Contactor Switchgear on 1st January 1951 - straight from school. For the first three months I worked in the stores, which was quite a good training as it familiarised me with all the components used in our products. After that I was transferred to the Machine Shop where I spent the next nine months. At the time I was sent to college on a one-day release and two evenings basis as part of my apprentice training. I had such a good report from the college that the management decided to offer me a vacancy that existed in the Test Department. So I worked for three months on simple testing, but seeing the finished panels is quite a different thing when you are expected to know what goes on inside them! I was still very much a trainee so I was moved to the Sub-Assembly Department, and at last all the knowledge I was gaining began to fall into place. I spent five or six years in that department, and learnt a little about the wiring, learning how to read wiring diagrams and schemes, and engineering drawings.

At Contactor we used to tailor-make equipment to the customer's requirements - we didn't really make finished items on a production line. It wasn't like making soap powder! There were certain standard components and standard lines we could make in reasonable quantities, but most switchgear was made to order, and we were proud of its quality - much of the equipment we made then is still working today - forty years later. I moved from assembly back into Testing and stayed there until 1959. The nature of the firm's work caused problems in maintaining its flow. We worked on a monthly basis and everything seemed to happen towards the end of the month as we tried to get evrything out. The last week of each month was panic stations, followed by a slack period as we waited for the next build up of work from the shop floor!

In October 1957 the firm celebrated its 21st birthday - and we we were all entertained at the directors' expense at a dinner at Wolverhampton Civic Hall. By then the company had almost six hundred employees. Typical of the family atmosphere of the business was the fact that we also had works' trips - but at the company's expense - not paid for by the Social Club like in some other firms.

By 1959 the company had become so big they decided to build a new works at Leominster in Herefordshire. I think they dreamed of building houses and establishing a company-based community out in the country. My father, who was foreman in the Sheet Steel Department, where we made our own panels and cases for the Switchgear was moved down to Leominster - so we all had to go! As it was still a new plant there was no Test Department, so I had to go back into stores work which I didn't like too much.

Within eighteen months I was back in Wolverhampton in the Test Department. Industry seemed to be booming and the testing had altered a little. We not only spent time calibrating thermal and magnetic overloads, we also tested spares. Spares now contributed to a large part of our trade. I also tested the contactors, setting the pole pressures and adjusting the cut outs - as laid down in the "Bibles" we had to work to, all worked out by the engineers and the Development Department.

It was a pleasure to go to work, because I enjoyed the job itself and the company of the workforce. If somebody left, we always asked in wonder, "Why have they gone?" Of course, like any other firm we had the "nomads" - people who just worked a year or two before moving on in search of experience. One of the first people I had the privilege of working with was Tom Storey, a staunch Trade Unionist from Tredeger, in South Wales. He negotiated a good bonus scheme with the company that added to our motivation. As well as his interest in the Labour Movement, he was Vice President of the Magic Circle in Wolverhampton and had useful show business connections that kept us well entertained at our thriving Sports & Social Club.

For a company that had prospered, and in which people were happy to work, the turning point came in 1969. From then on it was a "downhill slide". We were taken over by MTE. We had to stop making our own components and use theirs. The factory at Leominster was closed and 120 people were made redundant. Harry Rayner had already passed away and Jeanne Liwski was approaching retiremnt. MTE brought in their own directors.

We carried on until 1974, when MTE was swallowed up by a firm that made ball bearings - RHP. They decided to sell our original 1936 buildings and probably would have sold the lot had it not been for the fact that a Norwich firm, with which we had long done business, stepped in and saved us from closure. This was a large concern called LSE (Lawrence Scott and Electromotors). You can see how the workforce, many of whom had such long service, began to believe that however many take-overs we went through we would always survive. And depsite all the changes of name we still proudly thought of ourselves as the Contactor Switchgear. During the MTE period I had been tranferred to the Inpection Department - in which I worked for fourteen years.

In 1980 LSE became part of MS (Mining Supplies),

who already had a switchgear division, so we saw a few redundancies and the 1980s saw a recession gain momentum. By 1984 we were down to a workforce of about 120, but work seemed to be picking up slightly. There was even a little overtime that made people happy. The management was very loathe to make any pay rises, and if they did, it was balanced by further redundances. In 1985 they announced we would have to go onto a three day week - unheard of in the company's history. We were invited to take a gamble - work three days a week for three months and see if work picked up to avoid further redundances. We lost money by only working three days a week but we felt at least we were keeping our jobs.

That lasted from October 1985 until February 1986, and although we had lost out financially, we felt the gamble had paid off and work had picked up again. In July 1986 MS announced that we were to be sold off. These changes were always supposed to be well kept secrets but the shop floor could usually sense impending changes and accurately predict matters that we were not supposed to know anything about! Really you didn't need a degree to suspect what was going on. It is easy to spot rats deserting sinking ships!

On 1st July we had new owners and on 1st August it was announced that we would have to close and that everybody would finish on 31st October 1986. Some people, by then, had worked for the company for over forty years - and, as it turned out even the 120 of us still there were not going to survive that last three months. We were told that 36 of us had to be off the ground within a fortnight. If there was any argument the company would send in a "heavy gang" over the weekend to clear the factory. Take it or leave it.

We were all one hundred percent strong Trade Unionists but the Unions could do nothing - we believed the owners' threats. The Unions had four hours talks with the spokesman the new owners had sent to the factory - their "hatchet man", but he would only repeat the basic message. We gained one concession: if everybody co-operated they would give us £100 per ten years of service on top of our statutory redundancy pay. I had been there for thirty five years so I was being offered an extra £350 - providing everybody left as instructed without argument. There seemed to be nothing we could do. Even though we had been one big happy family this destroyed us. I had seen more of the lads at work than I'd seen of my own family over the thirty five years but now we were being played off against one another, in the sense that if one protested it could make it worse for others. I was a member of TASS, and I'm still a member to this day, but if the Union had put up a fight we stood to lose everything. I was in the first thirty six to go, so I finished on 15th August 1986.

One irony is that after we left the others had to work overtime to maintain production. That money earned in overtime was more than the "bonus" we were to receive once the closure was completed. We didn't let Contactor just fade away. We wound up the Sports & Social Club and used the money to put on a grand dinner at a local hotel for the last 120 employees and their wives, and a number of retired workers. Even the management put on a buffet on the final day that the firm was open and folks who had left up to thirty years earlier turned up for that! My father came back to Wolverhampton for the occasion - it was that important to us. Letters appeared in the Express and Star mourning the closure. I said earlier there was something of the phoenix about Contactor Switchgear, and sure enough, not only have many of us remained in touch with one another, but five chaps have started their own business - Contactor Controls!

Looking down Morfield Road from the offices of the Contactor Switchgear Co. at lunchtime. Capturing the atmosphere of the lunchbreak is a subject related to work that seems to have eluded most photographers, but this view has captured a few of the Switchgear staff taking the air, as well as showing the historic surroundings in which the factory grew up. In the distance is the building associated with the manufacture of

Sunbeam trolleybuses, occupied when this picture was taken, about 1953, by Villiers. Nearer on the left was the building occupied by Turner's. In 1989 it is still possible to photograph this view although the factories are now being turned into small industrial "units" and the skyline is now dominated by the Blakenhall Flats.
(Malcolm Palmer collection)

PURSLOW'S,
42, Bridge St., WEDNESBURY.

ESTABLISHED OVER PURSLOW'S CELEBRATED PORK PIES HOME MADE

60 YEARS PURSLOW'S CELEBRATED PORK PIES HOME MADE

HIGH CLASS BAKER AND CONFECTIONER

PURSLOWS CELEBRATED HOME MADE PORK PIES

MAKER OF THE CELEBRATED HOME-MADE
PORK PIES.

Sample 2 lb. Pie sent beautifully packed, post-free, for
1/9 P.O. or Stamps.

These Pies are **Famed throughout the District**
and form a most attractive delicacy.

Purslow's Pork Pies

Edna Vaughan

I started work in 1916, at the age of 13, at Purslow's Bakery, New Street, Wednesbury. My sister Elsie, who was a lot older than me, and who was married, already worked there. She spoke up for me and enabled me to get the job. When I started there were four of us women in the pie department, and three men in the bakery, working for the Purslows. We worked from seven till seven, Monday to Friday, and seven till two on Saturday, for a weekly wage of seven shillings. At that time, my father, who was a blacksmith, earned one pound three shillings a week. He gave my mother £1 per week for house-keeping, and the rest of the money was his to spend. Beer was then fourpence a quart, and if you needed a clay pipe, that was given free when you bought a quart of beer.

In those days we had a day's holiday on Christmas Day, Easter Monday, Whit Monday, and the first Monday in August. No one ever took a week's holiday because there wasn't any holiday pay. Each day we had a break at 9.30.am. for our snap, and later an hours lunch break. The people involved in the baking of bread and cakes had no fixed break as they had to wait until the ovens were empty. I remember when the Armistice was declared all the factories closed and everyone went to the market place to listen to the band, but we couldn't go because there was produce in the ovens cooking.

My special job was making pork pies which had to be hand raised. The gaffer put the flour in the trough, boiled up the fat, kneaded the flour and fat together into pastry and then weighed out the portions. I had to take the dough build it up like a cup round a wooden former. We rolled the dough and cut out the lids, and cut out the "flowers" - little pastry decorations added to the pies. The gaffer also weighed out the meat, and made the gravy by boiling up pork rind until it was jellied. The pies were baked in a coal-fired oven, which needed cleaning out after every bake. (Later this was gas-fired.) The bakery itself was lit by oil lamps. We also helped the men mix the bread dough, which was really hard work.

Most people were very poor, and during hard times pubs gave away grey peas and loaves. Although we worked in a bakery, things weren't any better: we were never allowed to take the damaged products - they all went into the pig swill bin. Stale cakes were sold in the shop at greatly reduced prices.

Mr.and Mrs.Purslow started the bakery on a shoe string and really had to struggle to get the business going. There was no money to pay for aprons, so we used empty flour bags, and we had to take them home to wash them. The struggle led to Mr.and Mrs.Purslow living in very mean circumstances, and this they continued to do even when things got better! There was no sickness benefit in those days, but one luxury they allowed was that if an employee was off sick, Mrs.Puslow would cook nourishing food and take it to them. Even if it was the husband, wife, or parent sick, she still sent a little food to help things along. But in their own home the fire was never lit, even in the winter, until the afternoon.

Mrs.Purslow's daughter, Hilda, made the cakes, for which we did the donkey work, and Mrs.Purslow's mother, who lived with them, came into the bakery every day. She brought her newspaper and sat by the ovens to keep warm. When the Purslows died within ten days of each other the business was left to their son and daughter. Hilda was an excellent business woman, but her brother was not really interested in it. They eventually sold out to Bradford's.

I worked there through two World Wars and did not retire until 1959, although I left for seven years in the 1940s. In the end I was making cakes for Bradford's, opposite the Albion football ground, but that was tedious compared with the variety of work I had done for Mr.and Mrs.Purslow. The work had been hard then but you got on with it whether you had backache or heartache!

The Last Place God Made

Joan Powderly

I grew up in Bilston and my Gran used to say, "Yo doh want to ever go to Bradley's. It's the last place God made!" Yet when I was about sixteen or seventeen I found myself starting work there. I started work on the hand presses, making buckets and mop buckets and all sorts. Then we went on to Bomb Tails and then to ironing boards. This girl and me made the first Beldray ironing board. It was going to be a four-year contract but its still being made now for all I

Miss Edna Halling, as she was then, at about the age of eighteen, while working at Purslows, photographed outside the front door of her home.

they were sent off all over the world. We were on piecework and the pair of us, jigging and spot-welding, could make eight hundred boards a day!

Sometimes they used to send a taxi for me on a Sunday to get me into work to get an order out on time - in time to catch the boat. And then, within a week or two we'd be sitting round doing nothing - back on basic and waiting to get another good order. It was when we were doing the eight hundred a day that we were really earning the money.

In hot weather you really used to sweat. It used to drip onto the work and all of a sudden you'd be spot-welding your sweat and you could hear it sizzle! We used to put about a hundred and fifty spots on ironing board. The shop next door used to bring them back if they weren't right or the welds had broken. If they brought them back to me I used to say, "My welds don't break like that." I knew it was the work of the girl next door because I could hear her welds going, I could hear them cracking. Eventually we used to put a spot where nobody else did so that we could always tell what work was ours. We could prove our work was good.

You had to learn the job as you went along. In fact, I can never remember learning - it just seemed as if you always knew. It's like swimming - once you could do it you felt as if you'd always been able to do it. At one stage I left, but after two years I went back to Bradleys again - to the same ironing boards! I worked there sixteen years altogether. I've still got a Mark III Beldray ironing board myself!

know. At the time we were a bit upset because we thought we weren't going to be paid piecework!

But, going back to the hand pressing, for a time I was making mop buckets. I was making the part where all the holes are - where you have to squeeze the mop, and making the flange that went into the bucket to be welded in place. I had to swing the hand press round three times. As I swung it round I was singing, "If I had my way dear,..." and then "Bonk", I'd put my head in the way! I had a lump on my head for three weeks. You had many a knock from those hand presses.

We always used to sing as we worked, although it drove the foreman mad. He used to say, "For God's sake, shut up!", but we used to reply, "That's the one thing you can't stop us doing - You can't stop us singing". Then he used to reply, "I wish I could!" But that was one way of getting rid of the boredom, because, basically they were boring jobs. We enjoyed work because there was a gang of us and we used to tease one another.

Making the ironing boards, I was a spot welder and jigger. It was hard work because you had to stand up all day at the bench, and your leg was going up and down, up and down, firing the welder. The spot welding machine was in the bench and you moved the board along. It came to us as a plain piece with all the holes blanked out. We had to start by putting the rim round the flat piece, but later they came with the rim already pressed. We had to weld the pieces in that held the legs. The jigger used to put the pieces in place and I'd spot weld - or we'd do it vice-versa. We stacked them up on a pallet, and after having their legs put on the boards went off to the spray shop. And then

Spot welding machines like this one were made in the Black Country. This model was made by Holden and Hunt of Old Hill.

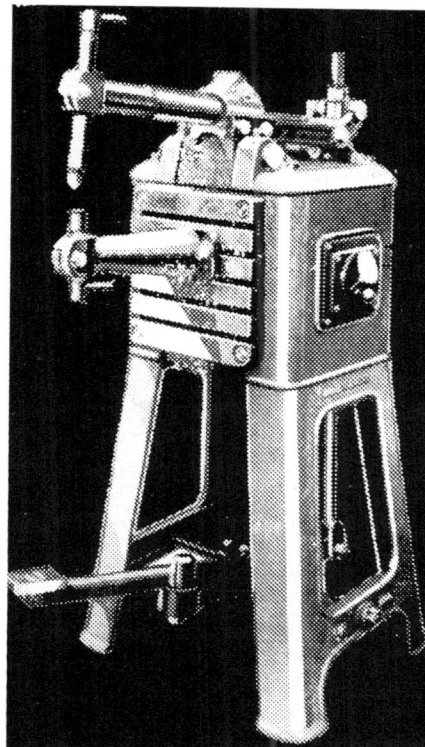

A Bit of Everything

Cyril Lord

I was born at the beginning of the century: August 1900, and I reckon I've done a bit of everything in the motor trade. But when I first left school I worked in Thomas Vaughan's pawn shop in Willenhall. (I'm Willenhall bred and born.) I used to write out pawn tickets - I've wrote as many as three hundred out on a Monday morning! For a few bob a week we worked long hours, sometimes it was midnight on Saturdays before we were putting up the thick wooden shutters of the shop.

In 1915 I was able to start an apprenticeship at Charles Richard, nut and bolt manufacturer in Darlaston. I think my parents paid for it to get me out the road. I worked there until 1923, learning all the skills of a general engineer - making tools, shaping, planing, turning. It was the most satisfying work I ever did. The thing I enjoyed most was fitting and turning - things like screw-cutting where there was some real skill involved. At Richard's I worked on a 10 swing centre lathe which stretched from wall to wall and had a chuck as big as myself. The lathes were all belt-driven - we had to reach up and put the belt on, and once, about 1919, I caught my hand under the belt. Nowadays all you do is press a button! We made the bolts for spiking chairs to railway sleepers - we had a special machine for making them, and sent them off to Wedge's at Willenhall to be galvanised. I also worked with Horsfall tools and press tools. By the time I was really skilled I could earn £2.15s (£2.75) a week but then I was seen off. You always got the sack when they had to pay you the top rate because there'd always be another apprentice to do the job. It was always, "Get your jacket on - and skite!"

I worked a short while at Wellman Smith & Owen and at Rubery Owen's foundry, casting cylinders for motors. By 1926 I was at the Clyno, in Wolverhampton, working nights for £3 a week. I was fitting up the front axles and assembling the cross steering. About six hundred men worked for Clyno at that time - they were an important car manufacturer, making about three hundred cars a week, in the works at Pelham Street, with the machine shop on one side of the road and the assembly shop on the other.

Then I got a job with Dundas & Dundas, the contractors building the new factory for Courtaulds in Wolverhampton. I was there from start to finish and I never had a day off - except for a fortnight when we were laid off because of frost. It took us six months to get the hole out, thirty feet down in the ground, to provide a base for the stack. We laid concrete floors and put up the steel work for the factory. It was the hardest I've ever worked. They used to expect six of us to carry those girders. If we were amassing bricks to ballast the crane they used to throw them at you two at a time - and you had to catch them! I had to fetch a man down from the jib of the crane once, but they never persuaded me to venture to the top of that stack. I believe it was 365 feet high, and two steeplejacks were killed building it. It was a disgrace that the place was ever demolished - it was a really well built factory.

In 1929 I joined the Willenhall Radiator and worked forty eight years there until I retired at the age of seventy seven. (I did leave and go to John Harper's foundry for a few months in 1940, but was soon back at the Radiator.) The firm was started by Harold Day, and was later run by his sons, Tony and Barry. At first there was only me, about four other men and some lads. There was no money and not much machinery. When there was no work in you had to have a night off. We worked at Temple Bar, in Willenhall, and did a bit of work for Sunbeam. I think it was a contract for Rover that made the firm, and later for Standard and Talbot. The firm moved to Bushbury for about three years and then to Neachell's Lane where the factory was built.

I did a bit of everything during my time but most of it was sheet metal work - beating wings and panels to shape with a hammer - not presswork like it is today! When we started making wings they had to be rolled through a rolling machine and then we shaped them - that was real skilled sheet metal work. At one time I worked nights from eight till eight and a night's work was drilling eighteen holes, with an electric drill, in fifty pairs of wings. We were skilled men but we didn't earn much - our wages barely came to £3 a week - and if you were caught washing your hands a minute before the time to finish they give you the sack -they'd say, "Put your clothes on..." Eventually wages improved after the War, largely due to the efforts of the union, I was in the AEU.

I did a few other things. For example I think I was the first to do some paint spraying there. I used to spray the Scammel cabs with red oxide undercoat. When we first moved to Neechell's Lane it was only a two bay factory but it grew to eight bays. I think they employed about two thousand people by the time I left. In 1977 they see'd me off. But I'd still like to do a bit of work now to take my mind off things!

5

PROVIDING SUPPORT

Generating Power.

John Downs

I started work at Ocker Hill Power Station in 1948, just after I had come out of the Navy. Fortunately while I had been in the Navy I had been in the engine rooms and boiler rooms and so it was really the same kind of work. At Ocker Hill I worked on "The Old Side" and they had very small turbines there.

I started in the basement as an A.P.A. - an auxiliary platform attendant, then I gradually worked my way up. My job was starting the turbines and there was quite a lot involved in that. You had to know about the steam side from the boiler room, the correct temperatures in the boilers, and the oil temperature had to be correct before the turbines started and went on load. I was very interested in both the turbines and the boilers.

At Ocker Hill they built a "New Side" about 1950 and I went onto that, on slightly bigger turbines. I rose to the position of charge hand - in charge of four turbines. Most important was the boiler feed pump pressure for the boiler house. I stayed there until it was eventually shut down about 1978 and I had to move to Walsall Power Station.

When I got the job it was the Midland Electric Power Company but I actually started on "vesting day" when it became part of the Central Electricity Generating Board. The CEGB was a very good firm to work for, and while we worked at the Power Station they encouraged us to study for our City and Guilds qualifications. The Board also sent us on summer schools.

We had good facilities and I played in a very good cricket team, playing down at Bailey's Lane, by the pool. Cricket balls were easily lost in the pool so we didn't count sixes - we played for fours! There was also a social club and even a Greenhouse Club where I learnt to grow tomatoes.

The worst times were during the winters when the cooling towers froze over. As the water went through the slats it tended to freeze up, so the Fire Brigade used to come to practice breaking the ice up. We also took burst oil-pipes very seriously and it was always a panic as we tried to prevent oil running into the canal. Later we had to take security very seriously. After the Birmingham Pub Bombings security became very intense and even the cable tunnels were closed.

Looking back now, one of the things I enjoyed were the "exchanges". For example for three months I went to Stourport Power Station. It was of great interest to me as every station had different turbines and boilers.

Inside the turbine Room at Ocker Hill Power Station in the 1950's. No. 2. Turbine is in the foreground, No. 1. in the background with gland steam blowing off. John Downs is standing, with his shirt sleeves rolled up, by the control panel. John still recalls being on the evening shift on the night of the last shut down – when the last ton of coal was burnt on the grate and the engineer sent for a bottle of whiskey to "celebrate" the shut down. (John Downs' collection)

Ocker Hill Power Station: the Turbine Hall is to the left of the building with four vertical stacks. The three cooling towers that were such prominent landmarks in the Black Country were demolished in 1985. Charles Dickinson (see page 74) worked on them while they were being built. (Collection of Keith Hodgkins)

The Drawing Office

Haydn Smith

I started work at Bayliss Jones & Bayliss Ltd., after the Second World War, as a junior draughtsman in the Fencing Drawing Office - so called to distiguish it from the Engineering Drawing Office. The F.D.O. was responsible for the design and production of working drawings not only for fencing but also for gates and architectural metalwork such as lanterns, war memorial plaques, inn signs and balustrades.

I remember the first day: it was a cold October morning and the office was situated apart from the main office and access to it was by means of an outside staircase. In the yard were some dejected prisoners of war who had not yet been returned to Germany. They were housed in the factory in a building on the opposite side of the yard. I felt rather depressed as I mounted that staircase. The office was a large old fashioned square-shaped room with a big fireplace. A long heavy table divided the room into two parts. On one side were about five draughtsmen and on the opposite side were about the same number of estimators. In the corner was a smaller office in which resided the Chief Draughtsman.

My initial depression soon evaporated since I was cordially accepted by the others and there was some good-natured banter exchanged between the draughtsmen and the estimators.

A considerable amount of work done in the office was for enquiries in which the drawing would be prepared with the estimate. Modifications often had to be drawn to keep down the price of the job. For the more prestigious jobs such as a pair of gates for a stately home or a Maharajah's palace, a water colour drawing would be prepared with a suitable background. On the other hand more mundane jobs were prepared from existing drawings, and ozalids, which were transparent prints, were made and modified to suit. Then opaque dye line prints were made. When each drawing was completed it would be entered meticulously into a large heavy book, resembling a family Bible. The entries were made in copperplate writing.

The customers were of all kinds. One that I remember was a children's author. He sent us the details of the items he wanted for his house, which included the weather vane and the letter included details of his exploits in climbing onto the roof to obtain measurements. It had all the drama and excitement of a short story!

Members of the sales staff would often go out and negotiate with clients and check their requirements. The head of that department was an ex Army Officer of the First World War - a gentleman of the old school. Apparently when negotiating with one customer he found that he had forgotten his measuring tape, so he measured the gate opening with his handkerchief. The opening was 15 handkerchiefs wide, but on his return to the office he could not remember whether he had used the length of the edge of his handkerchief or the diagonal. "Never mind," he exclaimed, "I'm going back tomorrow and I will ring you back confirming the measurements. The next day he phoned in confirming that the dimension was 15 handkerchiefs across the diagonals.

When the design and estimate was accepted by the client a working drawing would have to be prepared which was generally straightforward. However, when it involved ornamental iron work with scrolls and acanthus leaves these would have to be drawn freehand, and full-size, for the blacksmith. They were drawn with french chalk on thin metal sheets either on an easel, or in the case of large jobs, on several sheets laid out on the floor.

The ornamental castings would be made with wooden patterns, and often existing patterns could be utilized. This would entail searching for a suitable one in a large and dusty storeroom where the patterns that had been accumulated over decades were stacked on endless shelves. This was one job I detested. The Chief Draughtsman, whose father before him had held the same position, made models in clay of coats of arms and plaques which he cast in plaster of paris in his home workshop for the pattern shop. He was quite talented at this, but he lived in a world of his own, sitting in his office, smoking his pipe.

Occasionally he would emerge from his office, stretch himself, walk several steps back and forth with a detached expression in his eyes, clear his throat, check that everything was as it should be in the office, and then return to his own office to refill his pipe. During the day he would make an excursion to the main offices on the other side of the yard. One young draughtsman, who sat in the large bay window overlooking the yard, had rigged up a weird device using strings and mirrors by which means he could pan the yard and observe the approach of the Chief or any other V.I.P.

One day the Chief noticed this device and began pulling the strings with an air of naive curiosity. "What's this contraption for, Michael?" he asked. Fortunately Michael possessed sufficient presence of mind and fertility of imagination to extricate himself from this predicament. After a hesitant start he improvised a convincing, if convoluted, explanation that seemed to satisfy the Chief!

It was not all fun and games, however, and the work was not particularly well paid, and overtime was without extra pay. The only concession we received was a free tea which consisted of toast and jam with a pot of tea. I remember one night working until 9.30.pm., finishing off the drawing, printing it, and then posting it to the client on my way home.

One of the highlights of the social side of the firm was the annual Panto produced by the Amateur Dramatic Society in the staff canteen, in which both staff and factory joined in. A thousand and one tasks had to be undertaken to present a stage production: painting scenery, making costumes etc., as well as the acting. The Society also staged plays, at least one of which was presented at the Wulfrun Hall. The company had a very strong sports and social side to it and even published a monthly house magazine for everyone - produced to a very high standard. Today those magazines give a fascinating glimpse of the working lives and social lives of the Bayliss Jones & Bayliss employees.

I left the firm in the fifties, and afterwards, in the late sixties I believe the office closed down and draughtsmen were made redundant. Looking back to those days some forty years ago it is possible that time mellows the memory somewhat but, on the whole, those days seemed a happy period. It seems regrettable that in this modern age of plastics, high technology and computers that there appears to be no room for wrought iron gates and ornamental ironwork.

Haydn Smith's self portrait supplied to the Bayliss Jones and Bayliss monthly magazine

DANGER! MAN AT WORK!

The View from the Keyboard
Betty Crump

In 1947 I had the opportunity to leave Wrights Lane Central School, Old Hill, at the tender age of fourteen years. If I had been a couple of months younger I would have had to stay until I was fifteen. But as I was no lover of school (except for English and Art) I was only too eager to leave. No careers conventions, no hint of persuassion from any direction to remain at school came my way - so I was out. It was great. I enjoyed the Easter holidays without a care in the world and then set about looking in the local papers for work. Jobs were plentiful: one could pick and choose. I can remember thinking that I wouldn't work

S.W.BULLAS & SONS
LIMITED.

MANUFACTURERS OF ALL KINDS OF

GALVANIZED & JAPANNED STEEL HOLLOW-WARE.
TRUNKS FOR HOME & EXPORT. VARNISH, COLOUR & PAINT MAKERS.

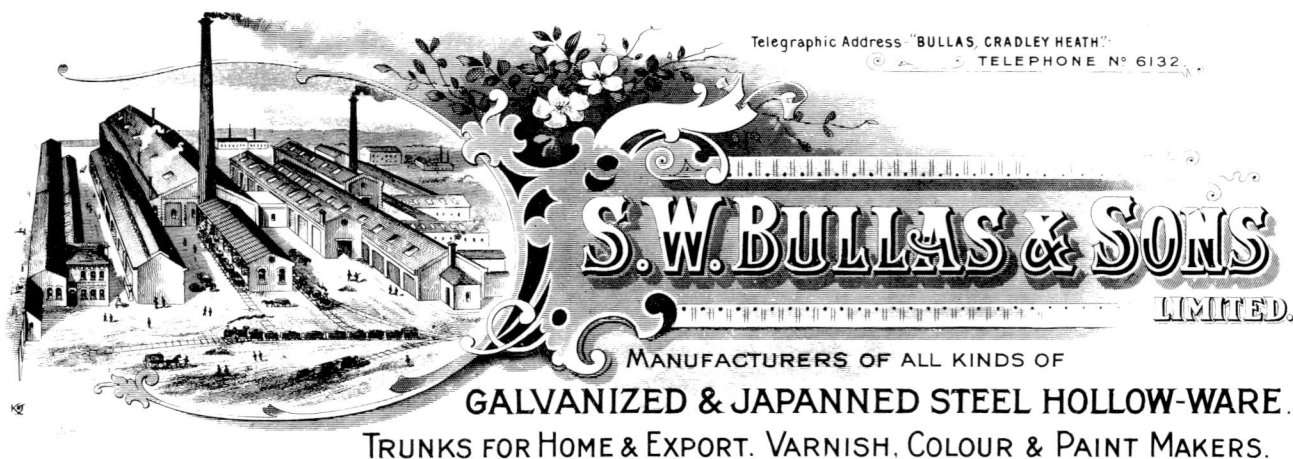

in a factory for a fortune. A shop maybe, but not a grocers or ironmongers, perhaps a rather "nice" dress shop or an office. The more I thought about office work, the more it appealed. I rather fancied myself pounding away on a typewriter. And so a week or so later I found myself working for Messrs S.W.Bullas & Sons Ltd., Corngreaves Road, Cradley Heath. They were paint manufacturers and steel metal workers, turning out an assortment of galvanized buckets, baths, etc., and black japanned officers' trunks.

The office was truly Dickensian in character. In the centre of the main office was a huge sloping desk which levelled out on top to accommodate inkwells, pens etc., and a foot or so above this was a rack on which could be found a multitude of papers and ledgers. These ledgers were enormous loose-leaf books which opened by means of a key whenever pages were to be added or taken away. This monster of a desk was reached by means of high stools, and once seated, there was a foot rest running along the length of it making it very comfortable when working away on the sloping surface, in fact, much more so than the low flat-topped tables I subsequently worked at. No one ever complained of backache at Bullas's. It was at this desk that I learnt book keeping.

There were four Bullas brothers in the business: Fred, Percy, John and Hugh. and ther were always addressed as Mr.Fred, Mr.Percy etc. Mr. Fred would be seated on a high stool to my right. Freda Gordon, a clerk, sat opposite me, Mr.John opposite left and Lily Cox, shorthand typist and wages clerk, opoposite right. If anyone was the office manager it was Mr.Fred, he was the eldest and most correspondence was signed by him. At first I was a little afraid of Mr.John, but as time went by I became used to this austere figure in the brown cow-gown. He was in charge of the galvanizing section. Mr.Percy was in charge of the Paints Dept. and Mr.Hugh in the Metalwork, but they had their own offices within their own parts of the factory.

To the rear of my section of desk was a flat topped table and the old Remington machine on which I typed; at first with two fingers and then, following a course of nightschool lessons, more proficiently. I typed invoices, letters etc., and when the monthly statements were typed we had had small adding machines which could be fixed to these typewriters and the amounts were typed in so that it could add them up. These were ingenious little gadgets - we called them "Totalizers". I've never seen one any-

where since. When we had a large consignment of goods ready there were often dozens of lables to be typed. this could be rather tedious, but once I had reached the 60wpm stage I really enjoyed typing on these thick cards, it made such a clatter and sounded like machine gun fire. It was a relief for the others when this noisy operation was over.

Occasionally I would have to go forth into the factory with a message for one of the brothers. As I passed through the metalwork section some of the fellows would embarass me with wolf whistles as I side-stepped dustbins, buckets, baths etc - all awaiting galvanizing. Galvanizing must have been a pig of a job. My recollection is of a large vat emitting the most evil of fumes. I never went very close - it wasn't so much the smell as the atmosphere. Even from a distance it was suffocating. The thin inconsequential articles would be lowered into this vat and come out bright and shining and looking very durable. I imagine the cost of a mere bucket was quite high in human terms.

The paint section is very hazy in my memory. I am sure one had to go up some steps to reach Mr.Percy's office, as if it were on stilts. It always seemed to be half empty but for a few drums of paint. I have a vision of Mr.Percy stirring the contents of one of these drums with a long stick. He was tall and thin and looked like a male witch attending his cauldron. His department was responsible for the japanning of officers' trunks, and these were stencilled with the owner's name.

Another member of staff was an elderly lady named Lizzie, who cleaned and made tea. I think it was Mr.Fred who had the idea of making sandwiches for the workers. Large joints of meat were purchased, cooked, sliced, and sold, and I can remember Lizzie coming into the office, when the coast was clear, telling us when a nice piece of beef was cooking, and asking who would like a round of bread dipped in the fat. Those squelching sandwiches were delicious. No one spoke of cholesterol in those days!

I wouldn't have missed working for this old fashioned family business for the world - even though it did have some disadvantages. For example, in the winter a coal fire would be blazing away (if we were lucky) in the fireplace on the opposite side of the office to where I sat. It was all of 45 degrees around my feet. I always had chilblains in the cold weather and was glad when summer came. After four years with S.W.Bullas & Sons I decided to move on. But things were never quite the same anywhere else!

Oiling the Wheels of Industry

Alex Chatwin

In August 1942 I started work in the laboratory of Messrs.Gaunt & Hickman Ltd., British Oil Works, Monmore Green, Wolverhampton. The firm, a private company, supplied lubricants to the South Staffordhire coal mining industry as well as many engineering and transport companies. It had been formed in 1848 with premises on the Old Heath Road and later in Molineux Street, moving to the Bilston Road site on the Birmingham Canal in 1911. A descendant of one of the founders, Mr.Fred Hickman, an elderly gentleman, came into the office occasionally, but it had been his elder brother, Mr.Moore Hickman, who had died a few years earlier, who had been the driving force in establishing the laboratory and putting the company's production on a scientific basis. He had been a graduate of Birmingham University in the early days and was a pioneer in the development of soluble cutting oils. The principal shareholder, and Company Secretary, Mr.Sydney Snow, now controlled the business. I remember him telling us how his father, in the nineteenth century, had sold the company's products to the small gin-pits and drift mines in the Black Country. These were small family businesses and he had collected payment from the wives of the owners who lived in cottages near their pit heads.

The principal raw materials, lubricating oils of various viscosities and qualities, came in the main from the Shell refinery at Stanlow near Ellesmere Port. The oil arrived in railway tankers of 10-14 tons capacity at Monmore Green Basin on the LMS system. There the tankers were emptied into one of the two narrow boats owned by the company. One of these, an old tar boat with three compartments, had a small vertical boiler mounted at the rear. This enabled the oils to be heated via steam coils in the railway tanker and the narrow boat, to facilitate pumping. The other vessel, an open "monkey boat", had been fitted with a long cylindrical tank, unheated, for use with the lighter oils. When full, these boats were poled under the Bilston Road bridge, and their cargoes pumped into the company's storage tanks.

The office staff consisted of Mr.Snow, an office manager, a representative, and about four lady clerks and typists. The works was staffed by a Works Manager/Chemist, myself, a foreman, a fitter, a cooper, about five labourers and three drivers.

Lubricating oils were blended in tanks with electric stirrers, heated by steam jackets or coils, or in smaller vessels directly heated by coal fires. Steam was provided by a coal-fired Lancashire boiler. One very obvious difference compared with today's practices was the use of manual labour. There were no fork lift trucks, and barrels had to be man-handled up wooden "skids" to be emptied into the tanks. One of the company's main products was black "tub grease" or "corve grease" which was used in all the mines to lubricate the axles of the coal tubs drawn by pit ponies. This grease contained a rosin oil, the manufacture of which was a closely guarded secret. At this distance of time, "all can be revealed". We reacted several tons of wood rosin with Flowers of Sulphur at a high temperature in a large coal-fired pot "still". Considerable volumes of hydrogen sulphide were released into a tall brick chimney. This process was used about twice a year and there were usually complaints in the local press about the disgusting smell, as far away as Walsall and Wednesbury.

The same fire heated still was used to manufacture "Bronze Oil", a varnish-like rust preventative formulated with various gums and linseed oil dissolved in petroleum solvent.The fire and explosion hazard must have been very real but no-one seemed to bother. This "Bronze Oil" was used in large volumes by our neighbours - Bayliss Jones & Bayliss to coat the threaded spikes they made for holding down the metal "chairs" on to railway sleepers, and also the spindles which held the pot insulators on telegraph poles.

There were few chemical additives to improve the basic oils in those days, but we used a wide variety of animal and vegetable fats such as tallow, lard oil, whale oil, rapeseed oil and linseed oil. The place was alive with rats!

For the size of the company, the laboratory was very well equipped, and after an initial spell of bottle washing, I was instructed in the basic testing procedures and chemical analysis of lubricants. I attended Technical College on three evenings a week plus half a day's release from work. Looking back, the laboratory also contained its hazards; principally a large coke stove, as well as gas burners used in close proximity to inflammable solvents. Occasionally there were small fires, but luckily nothing serious.

Lubricating oils were sold in five and ten gallon drums as well as 40-45 gallon drums. There were no meters for measuring, so each large drum had to be weighed empty and full, and the tare, nett and gross weight stencilled on the end. No two drums contained the same amount so there was much laborious work in recording each weight, and invoicing the volume as so many gallons calculated at an arbitrary nine pounds to the gallon. Greases were despatched either in galvanised buckets of 28lbs. or in wooden barrels. The cooper was kept busy repairing barrels, tightening hoops, and fitting new heads, after each trip.

We had two road tankers, but most products went out in barrels. To assist in loading, flat lorries backed down into a pit so that the barrels could be rolled on at ground level, but the gradient out of the pit was too much for the shire horses used with the railway companies' drays, and they had to be helped by a motor vehicle pulling with a rope. The horses then came up at the gallop with sparks flying from their hooves.

On Friday afternoons I exchanged my white laboratory smock for a boiler suit and proceeded to dip all the storage tanks so that new supplies could be ordered for the following week. A few of the tanks had fixed steel ladders, but for the rest I used a wooden ladder which I carried around. Some of the interior tanks were vertical cylinders without tops and I had to balance on the edge, holding on to pipes etc., while lowering the dipstick. A fall into ten feet of lubricating oil did not bear thinking about.

I stayed with the company until 1946 and then moved on to other parts of the oil industry. It was good foundation to my career, and even now, nearly fifty years later, I occasionally need some bit of technical "know-how" that I learned in the 1940s at Gaunt & Hickman Ltd.

Up In The Air - In A World of Your Own.

Charles Dickinson

I came to the Black Country in 1920 - when I was 4 years old. We came from Hanley, and after the First World War my father walked to this area in search of work. He was a shingler and he found work at Bagnall's Iron & Steel Works, Lea Brook, Wednesbury. Some of my brothers also worked there and I worked there for a time. My first experience of work, after leaving school at fourteen was chopping and bundling firewood. I had to wait a fortnight for my first money - 7/6 (37ãp) and only stayed for three weeks altogether! the I worked at the Triplex Foundry in Tipton, in the warehouse stores, for about eight months for ten shillings a week. After that I followed my father's and brothers' footsteps to Bagnalls.

I worked in the srcrap yard, working a forty eight hour week for ten shillings. Then, at the age of fifteen I started trolleying balls of metal from the furnaces to the hammer - to be hammered out to go under the rolls. It was hot metal and could weigh between one and two hundredweight. We used a steel fork truck, on two wheels, and had to pull them and shove them to put the metal onto the anvil of the big steam hammer. One day I fell backwards when I was drawing from the furnace and tripped. I had to wait two and a half hours in the office to be taken to hospital to have seven stitches in my arm. The trolleying work was the kind of thing that lads had to do before going on to other things, but I left before tackling anything else.

At that time it was difficult to find work and I was not sure what I should set out to do. I started work at Charles Lathe's and made tiled fireplaces for three years until fate set me off in another direction when I was nineteen. I had a brother two years older than myself who was killed in a motorcycle accident. Shortly afterwards I was offered his old job at Tildesley's Structural Steel Works and for the next eight months I was introduced to the world of steel erecting.

So - in 1936 I became a steel erector, and that was my job for most of my working life. I worked for a number of firms - Horsley Piggott's, Braithwaite's, and Chatterway's but most often I worked for Norton Harty of Great Bridge, and for Wright's Forge of Tipton (Boiler Division). A great deal of my life has been spent erecting colliery head gear, screening plants and washeries. Each time the work only lasted for the duration of the job, but I was never out of work for long. It was a satisfying job - I used to love it, and one of the things I liked most about my working life was travelling all over the country meeting different people.

The strange thing is that, as a child, I wouldn't walk on the kerb for fear of falling off. Yet in my working life I liked the element of risk and danger in the job. When you are up in the air you are in a world of your own. The danger was inherent in the job - when we put up the steelwork we didn't have ladders or scaffolding. We simply climbed, like spiders, up the steelwork itself. We had to catch hold of the flanges of the stanchions, put our knees inside the flanges and our feet outside to grip and then just start "walking up". On our belts we had what we called "frogs" to put our spanners in, and our hammer. We carried our bolts in one side pocket, and the drifts in the other.

When I had climbed the stanchion to where I was working I put my podge spanner in the one hole, put the drift into the other and hammered it in so that the bolt could be put in. The drift, a four inches long piece of steel with tapered ends cleared the hole for the bolt to go through. Once one bolt was in, it was possible to sit on the girder and work. There was little you could do for protection. Gloves would have been in the way when you were using the hammer and the drifts. If you were working with two "old hands" they could make it very difficult for you to get your bolts in. They would get theirs in first and make it difficult for you at the other end of the girder! It was best when there was good teamwork from the men at each end. Another danger was that we had to be at our place on the stanchion before the girder was swung into position so that we could help land it. Sometimes we had to thread it between the flanges of the stanchion before we could bolt it in position. It was possible to be knocked off the steelwork. Two men working with me were knocked off the frame at Cannock Wood Colliery. One broke his legs, the other injured his back and fractured the back of his skull.

Not only did we erect steelwork without the aid of ladders or scaffolding but we also had no cranes. The first job to be done on site was to erect a derrick. The tallest derrick we had was one hundred feet and was made in five sections that had to bolted together while on the ground. Then it was raised with winches and held aloft by four guy wires attached to crab winches which were staked down and weighted in place with old bricks. The highest headgear on which I worked was 140 feet at Barnburgh Pit, in Yorkshire.

After we erected the steelwork we did sometimes put up scaffolding for rivetters to work, and it was our job to put components in place for the fitters to complete the installation, such as screens and winding wheels. Collieries often provided their own labourers to complete the job and these were some of the wonderful characters that I met. At Highley Colliery the youngest labourer was 57 and the oldest was a 72 year old rope-splicer. There was a sixty seven year old who was so strong that nobody would work with him underground - he would have worn them out! They fetched and carried the girders and did the concrete mixing.

I first got a job with Norton Harty because my father-in-law was a foreman there - Harry Tranter - he was a real master of steel erecting and he taught me a great deal. It was good to work under him on four or five jobs. One of the first jobs we did was down at Baggeridge Brickworks, putting in some conveyors from the kilns to the loading bays. Then, just before the War, we were taken down to Himley No.4 - just behind the Crooked House, to build a new plant.

The pit had been abandoned after flooding but they wanted to bring it back into use. An old fellow who had once worked in the pit used to come down every day and see how we were getting on. He always said that we would never be able to reopen it. One day the ganger got really annoyed and told him to get off, but the engineer took him seriously and wanted to know why it would never reopen. The old man was right - No.4 had to be abandoned again! We went to install a Dry Cleaning plant at Baggeridge Colliery - it was supposed to clean the coal in a dry state but that failed after the first couple of shifts and was demolished! At Hamstead Colliery, and then Jubilee, we put in new screening plant and washeries. Although I worked at many pits and talked with many colliers, I never went underground. I always thought to myself, I'd rather be up in the air. I had a sense that I would be in danger if I went underground.

For a time during the War I left Norton Harty and joined Wright's Forge. The boiler erection side - the "Barley Yard" was on the far side of the canal to the main works. We built and installed coal-fired gas producers. Some of this was local work, for example at Chance's in Oldbury, and we took down part of the old Tipton Furnaces and erected them at Bloxwich, but much of the work was away. I worked at Sellafield for eleven weeks - and it rained non-stop for the whole time! We worked as a gang of five men and a foreman, and earned 1/6ā an hour. After ten years of steel erecting I was in charge of a gang myself. One thing I found was that if a problem arose I could usually solve it the next day - as if I had dreamt the solution.

Although I liked the work, and met many interesting men on my travels, in the end I decided I wanted a bit of home life. I got a job at W. Wesson's, Bull Lane, Moxley on maintenance and worked there until I retired. It was interesting watching men roll the steel. I had to get used to being at home and working in one place but I found family life comfortable. If I had my time all over again its hard to say whether I would want to do the same again. In my time I've broken both my big toes, I've broken my ankle, and I have had the tendon ripped out of my left thumb - and had to have thirty three stitches. But my father and brothers did not fare better at Bagnalls. My oldest brother had his heel burnt off while pulling a trolley of molten metal from the furnace. Another brother was crushed in a machine. My father scalded his back very badly in the thirties and had to take a labouring job - it broke his heart. I travelled the country, and met a lot of different people, and enjoyed being up in the air on the steelwork.

Road and Rail transport are an aspect of the working world that are generally well photographed although the subject of such photographs tend to be machines rather than men. Like other workers, transport workers do not often take a camera to work with them (with some notable exceptions). However, the late Paddy Powderly, a brick archer at Stafford Road, Wolverhampton, took his camera to work on several occasions just after the Second World War, and made a fascinating visual record of his workmates. In this instance Paddy stepped into the picture himself and is second from the right. On his left are Jim Carney and Alf Roberts, on his right is Harry Jacobs. The men are boilersmiths and fitters. Even the man on the footplate of GWR 0-6-OPT 3760, Jack Cavanagh, is a boilersmith, not a footplateman as you might be tempted to think! In his single days, when he first joined the railway, Paddy lodged in the railway hostel with Jimmy Donellan, a fellow Irish emigre. Forty years later it was Jimmy who was able to identify all but one of the men in this photograph, and could vividly recall Paddy's ability to slip into a locomotive's firebox while it was still warm to work on the brick arches that formed the grate. (The photograph comes from the collection of Joan Powderly, who recalls her own work as a spot welder earlier in this book.)

6

ON THE MOVE

Footplate Memories

Reg Share

Reg Share was born at the beginning of the century and began his railway career during the First World War as a cleaner at the London & North Western Railway's shed at Bescot. He died in July 1981, but had recorded some of his railway memories in 1978 for Jack Haddock, who has made these two tales available for this book.

The Wednesbury Shunt Duty

The Wednesbury Shunt was one of Bescot's engine-men's duties from the day the shed opened until the end of steam. It involved shunting duties in the sidings at Wednesbury Town Station, and the sidings that served the Patent Shaft Steel Works, as well as sidings along the single track line between Wednesbury and Darlaston (James Bridge) and the exchange sidings to the GWR. The locomotive had to be available virtually 24 hours and therefore left Bescot at 5.00.am. on Monday and remained at Wednesbury until the following Saturday afternoon. A coal wagon was provided at Wednesbury Goods Yard, and the night shift fireman had to coal up the engine.

Towards the end of the First World War there was a severe shortage of manpower on the railways. I was only a seventeen year old cleaner and, in normal times would not have expected to go on the footplate until twentyone, but I found myself made fireman and allocated to this particular duty. The manpower shortage also led to men being retained well past their normal retiring age, which was 70 at that time. As there was no substantial pension men often claimed to be younger than they were simply to go on drawing a wage for as long as possible. Thus a raw 17 year old found himself mating Mr. Hobley-Grey who was probably well into his eighties!

The first thing I learned was that Hobley-Grey's eyesight was such that he could barely see past a distance of about ten wagons. I had to guide him verbally most of the time, and he quickly taught me to drive the engine so that I could unofficially take on that duty in bad light or at night - while he did the firing! My inexperience with the regulator of the Webb 0-6-2 tank engine soon caused problems.

I misjudged my speed on approaching some wagons and the shunter, taken by surprise, had his shunter's pole knocked from his grasp. It cracked him on the jaw and laid him out flat. When he came round he made for Hobley-Grey, assuming the driver was responsible, and admonished him in a torrent of four-letter abuse in best Black Country style. The old man had to take it, knowing that if he admitted that he had let the lad drive the engine the shunter might report it and he would be finished for good. Afterwards he gave me a gentle talking-to.

My duties included maintaining fuel and water supplies for the engine, but I soon discovered I also had keep the old driver topped up with best bitter and cheese sandwiches from a local pub. Hobley-Grey explained to me, "That's what makes a steam shunting engine go, Reg: coal, water, bread, cheese, and best bitter." He explained many other things to me. For example, as we passed under the Holyhead Road, he told me that fresh clear air from North Wales blew straight down that road to help purify the air of the Black Country.

Once while taking on water we caused ten minutes delay to the Dudley-Walsall local passenger train, which was a cardinal sin, and Hobley-Grey was carpeted by the management and was given numerous forms to fill in. I found that my duties extended to helping fill them in. I thought I had grasped just about how wide my duties were until taken by surprise yet again on the night shift. Hobley-Grey came onto the footplate with a large wooden box and a bucket. He sat down on the box and asked me to open the firebox door. As I did so he took his boots and thick woollen socks off, and placed one foot on the upturned bucket. Out of his pocket he took a cut-throat razor and asked me if I would be so kind as to cut his corns. As far as I knew this duty was not specified in the LNWR regulations but I felt sorry for him, so I said, "O.K. - but I have never held a cut-throat razor before. What if I cut your toes off?"
He retorted, "I wish you bloody well would - it would save me some pain!"

I was his fireman for almost a year, but as the War ended men returned to their civilian jobs. It spelt the end for Hobley-Grey, and I had to go back to engine cleaning at Bescot. I did not go firing again until 1922.

A Trip to Willesden

One Bescot duty used to be the daily working of four heavy coal trains to Wilesden Junction, taking domestic coal from the Cannock Chase Coalfield to London, and returning empty wagons. It was a double trip for our men as Willesden men did not work those trains. The up trip was a most gruelling task for the men on the footplate, especially the fireman. On most trips the train ran with 55 loose-coupled coal wagons, and it took the slow line via Northampton.

One night, in November 1925, I was working the 2 till 10 shift. I was a senior shed cleaner awaiting promotion to the first link fireman's duty, and my firing experience was limited to local shunting turns. A Willesden train was supposed to leave at 8.10.pm. but the booked fireman failed to turn up. The shed foreman, Jack Rowley, had to find a spare-link fireman, but to his consternation he found they all had jobs. As he toured the shed he came across me and

Towards the end of the fifties the coal from the Cannock Chase Coalfield was still being taken to Willesden, via Bescot, in trains hauled by the same LNWR 0-8-0 locomotives that had provided a footplate initiation for the young Reg Share, as described here. The indefatigable Jack Haddock has captured 49126 bringing the train round the curve from Walsall (Pleck Junction) into Bescot. The line on the left curves round to Bescot Curve Junction on the Walsall-Dudley line. Trains still traverse these tracks but photographs are unlikely to record the fact as this location is now right underneath the M6 motorway!

promptly instructed me to clean the footplate of class G1 0-8-0 no.9045 - and to raise steam. I was told the call-up lad would inform my parents and I was loaned half a crown to buy myself food at Willesden Barracks. I had been at work five hours and could now look forward to another ten hours, little knowing that it was to be the make or break point of forty seven years service on the railway!

Whilst I was busying myself on the footplate Driver Tom Ellison suddenly confronted me. "Where is my mate?" he exclaimed. When I explained that I was his mate he shot off to find the shed foreman. After some argument it was agreed that if I failed to maintain a good supply of steam, or work to the required standard of footplate cohesion, I could be replaced at any of the sheds en route. As we left his only advice was, "Watch the steam gauge and keep up the boiler pressure." As I had never worked further than Aston there was no point in trying to assist in watching for signals, so all I did was shovel coal.

We thrashed off into the night, making a distinctive firework display with red hot char ejected from the chimney - sometimes almost reaching a speed of twenty miles per hour. I continued to shovel. We passed straight through Rugby, and even though it was downhill to Northampton I still had to keep on shovelling. Well after midnight we arrived in Bletchley Sidings and queued up behind other London-bound freight trains pausing for wheel inspection. I had no idea where we were. I was allowed to have a short rest and make a can of tea. I asked if we should uncouple the train and retire to the shed - I thought we had reached Willesden. Tom said that Willesden was still some fortyfive miles away - and another two hours of hard firing.

We did eventually arrive at Willesden and I barely had strength to uncouple the train. We ran onto Willesden Shed and handed our engine over to the disposal men. I followed Tom to the Railway Barracks, but as we arrived he disappeared without any explanation of the routines I should follow. The residents told me to take my snap to the mess room, but I had no food. I used my half crown to buy some bacon and

eggs from a local shop - to be immediateley cooked and eaten. I found a bed and was told I would be called at 4.30.am. We set out for Bescot at 6.30.am. with 55 empty coal wagons.

Although the return trip was easier, there was no respite for me. The driver gave me no help or advice, save to keep firing and keep the steam up. This resulted in the safety valves continually "blowing off" and by the time we reached Rugby I felt I had to protest. I suggested we were wasting steam, as it seemed to be a down-hill trip. The driver replied, "You bloody young fool, the World is round and it's always up to us to reach the top, so keep on firing and don't ask questions." At approximately midnight we passed Newton Road signal box to be routed through Bescot Sidings to the No.5 end sidings.

I uncoupled the engine and a few moments later it came to rest on the disposal road. I felt as if I had been away from Bescot for years, instead of some twenty four hours. I returned the tools to the stores but the driver disappeared. some of the shed staff were saying things like, "Wait till you get a hard job...."

I rose early to rejoin the 2.00.pm cleaning shift but when I booked on I was in for a surprise. The clerk informed me I was again working with Driver Ellison - taking a goods train to Edge Hill on another double duty. To my amazement, right from the departure point, Driver Ellison was a different man, giving advice about methods of firing, being helpful and talkative, and, above all, being friendly and making me feel one of a team! At Edge Hill Barracks he helped with the Barrack Room system and made me feel at home.

Tom Ellison later explained to me that the school of thought that prevailed on the LMS in the twenties was "throw a man in the deep end". My trip to Willesden was a make-or-break initiation to see how I would cope. Having survived that, Driver Ellison decided that I had the makings of a fireman, and gave me encouragement and helped me gain confidence. I decided it was worth staying on the footplate, and, in fact worked at Bescot Shed for a further forty seven years.

On and Off the Track

Jack Griffiths

At the age of ten, while I was still at school, I went as an errand boy to a draper's shop in the Lye and did that for three years. In 1920, when I was thirteen I left school and was promised a job in a nail warehouse, but it never came off. The summer of 1920 was a good one and I did some hay-making for my Uncle, who was a farm bailiff. There I ran into the chainmakers. After they had done a morning's work they used to go hay-making in the afternoon and evening. Then I managed to get a job in a coal merchant's office until the manager's nephew wanted the job and I was pushed out. I went to Baker's, the horse shoe factory in King Street, Lye. It's still there today, and the machine I worked on in 1924 is still working today! In 1924 I applied for a job on the railway.

When I joined the railway I expected to be given an office job, but instead I was given the job of "slipper lad" - the lad who worked with the shunting horses, putting trucks in position in private sidings where engines could not go. The job was at Stourbridge Basin - putting wagons in position for the boat traffic, of which there was quite a lot in those days. There were also sidings for Turney's, Eveson's wagon works and the sand siding. We had two horses, which we had to clean out and which had to be kept clean and tidy. A Horse Inspector used to come round and he would go down the side of the horse with his hankerchief - if there was any dust on it you were in for a good row. A travelling farrier used to come once a month to shoe the railway horses, with shoes he had already made to size. Every so often we had to load up a wagon with

Jack Griffiths sees off a special train of lady passengers in the role of Enquiry Inspector at Birmingham New Street Station about 1970, towards the end of a long railway career that began in 1924 at Stourbridge Town Local Goods Yard. Local railwaymen have a tradition of playing a part in the political life of the various Black Country communities. Jack Griffiths, known as "Doc" on the railway, was Mayor of Stourbridge 1962-63. (Photo: Birmingham Post)

the horse muck to be despatched to Evesham to be sold off. I started when I was fifteen and a half and stayed there until I was twenty.

At the age of twenty you started earning a man's wage, and I was offered a job at Hockley as a porter in the Transhipment Shed. We worked in gangs of four porters, one caller-off and a checker seated at his desk. One of my duties was to help the clerk with the payment of wages. I was able to recognise and identify everybody and could therefore check that no one was coming up twice and claiming somebody else's money! I also had to evaluate a porter's truck that Metalisation of Dudley were offering the railway. I had to try it out, compare it with the traditional railway barrow and write a report on the matter.

It was shift work, which I didn't like, so I transferred to Soho and Winson Green Mileage Yard where I gained experience with a great variety of traffic from petrol to beer. In 1930 the milk trade changed as milk bottles came onto the market. Handsworth Dairy decided to have a bottling plant and bottles arrived from St. Helens, just laid in layers in ordinary open wagons. After I had been there a couple of years the railway received Government money to build a warehouse under a scheme to relieve unemployment. I watched the warehouse being built and dealt with a variety of traffic in it. Mars started at about that time and I remember a fortnight when we had nothing but vanloads of Mars Bars arriving in plain cartons, and then the orders came in and we had to consign them to the local shopkeepers. We stored barley for the brewery - stacked by hand. We were expected to move ninety tons of barley for a day's work, and earned a penny a ton for any weight moved after that ninety tons! From portering I progressed to capstan shunting.

By then the War had begun and I was transfered to Langley Green where the shunter's duties even included issuing tickets on one turn. For a time I was a temporary Goods Guard but I had to come off the trains to pursue promotion. I became Head Shunter at Stourbridge Junction and then went back as a permanent Goods Guard for eight or nine years, during which time I had several adventures.

While I was a Goods Guard I had the experince of being run-into in Dudley Tunnel. It was June 1950, and I was showing some LMS men from Saltley the road between Stourbridge Junction and Dudley. As we went into the tunnel the LMS chaps asked what it was like. I explained that it was quite long and that a signal at the far end often halted the train with the guard's van still in the tunnel. Sure enough we stopped for about half a minute. We had just started and felt the "snatch" as the lose-coupled wagons started to move off, when I heard a GWR diesel railcar coming up behind us. There was a hell of a bump, but we were moving, and just at that moment we came out into the daylight. As the diesel railcar hit us I could see the driver's face through his windscreen!

The van derailed and ran up on to the end of the platform at Dudley as I could hear Bill Taylor, the signalman, shouting, "I've got the diesel behind you, Jack!" I shouted back, "He bloody well hit us!" and we ran back down the line to see what had happened. The driver, Billy Robbins, had brought the railcar to a halt, had got his passengers out and they were sitting on the bank at the end of the tunnel.

On another occasion I was on a runaway between

Dudley and Great Bridge with a train of copper ingots. It was roughly a one in seventy grade and the train was over-running the engine. I opened the sand and screwed the hand brake on but we still tore down past Palethorpe's Siding. The driver was Chanty, Harold Chant, and somehow, as we went through Great Bridge, he managed to put the engine into reverse and brought us to a halt just before Eagle Crossing! In the opposite direction I also encountered trouble with a train being banked from Great Bridge to Dudley. We came to a halt on the bank and I had to split the train by leaving some wagons in Palethorpe's Siding which was a tricky manouvre.

I eventually applied for the post of Goods Yard Foreman at Dudley, which was another step in promotion but I lost money by it, as I didn't get overtime anymore, and it was back to eight hour shifts. In the job you were a buffer between the LMS and the Great Western. Although it was an exchange point between the two companies there was only one Yard Foreman - to manage two administrations. If, for example, you refused train 807 on the LMS they would be on the phone within the hour saying that 809 was on its way. It was really the same train renumbered, and you had to cope with it as best you could.

One day at Dudley I had to re-rail two engines, which is a bit of a record. An engine had brought the perishable traffic, usually bananas, from Oxley, and was reversing from the Up road to the Down when it split the points, derailing the bogies. We managed to re-rail it. That evening the Station Master came up to me to announce that an LMS engine had done the same thing, and de-railed the pony wheels. Luckily both engines were in the hands of good drivers and they knew how to get them back on the track. Once the diesel railcar on the Dudley - Birmingham service crossed the road and the signalman changed the point while the railcar was over it. We had one bogie on one road and the other bogie on the other! An Inspector who was present said, "I don't like the look of this, I'm off to Old Hill!" Left to it I managed to find some chain and with the help of the shunting engine we put matters right.

I came back to Stourbridge Junction as the "Spiv" Inspector - Rest Day Relief work in the three shunting yards, and also relieving the Platform Inspector. All three yards, the North End, the Middle, and the Back were very busy and there was a lot of banking work involved, assisting trains up to Dudley and up Cradley Bank - so there was plenty to occupy my mind!

When Stourbridge MPD closed in 1967 I found myself back shunting as Chargeman rather than face redundancy. They eventually found me a job as Enquiry Inspector at Birmingham New Street, a position from which I retired in 1972 - two years short of fifty years on the railway.

Corporation Transport

Alan Butler.

I started work for Wolverhampton Transport in 1924 as a seventeen year old errand boy. Unemployment was very bad then - there was no work to be had and no question of any apprenticeships. I had been doing a bit of sweeping up for a firm in Horseley Fields but someone told me they wanted tram conductors. You could become a tram conductor at 18.

I wrote to the Transport Department, to Mr. Silvers, and told a lie - saying that I would be nineteen shortly, and I was sent for. I was interviewed by chief Inspector MacDonagh, one of Nature's fine gentlemen. He said that I couldn't be a tram conductor, but meanwhile I could have a job as an errand boy, driving a motorcycle and sidecar. I would have to take inspectors out to various parts of the system, to place bets at the bookies, and fetch beer from the pub for the fitters when nobody was looking. I would have to clean the fitters' benches and sweep the floor and generally be a handy sort of bloke.

When I did become old enough they taught me conducting on a part-time weekend basis, when other drivers and conductors were off. They taught me tram driving but legally I was not old enough to do that. But it was useful for me to be able to drive a tram in an emergency, and there used to be a tram that washed out the tram track, flooding it with water, I could drive that. Occasionally I was able to drive the pay tram from the depot in Cleveland Road into Victoria Square - into the middle of the road, where the staff came to collect their wages.

My tram driving experience was limited because they were going off the road at the time, but they also taught me the job on trolleybuses. The first trolleybus had operated in Wolverhampton in 1923 before I joined the Transport Department. I learnt to drive a trolleybus on the Tilling Stevens solid tyred vehicles. Mr. Silvers had patented a foot control system with which to drive a trolleybus, pressing a pedal with the left foot. Just to confuse matters Guy Motors built some vehicles controlled with the right foot. This left our hands free to take the steering wheel instead of a tiller.

I remember the first Guy double decker, number thirty, with an open staircase at the rear. If you weren't very careful you went over the back!

From about 1929 onwards I was loaned to Sunbeam on trolleybus test and development. Sunbeam built a six wheel chassis and placed a cabin in the centre for the test engineers, about seven tons weight at the back to keep the rear end down, and off we would go on the Wolverhampton - Dudley road, as far as Sedgley Bull Ring, carrying out speed tests, brake tests and current consumption tests. When we returned to Dudding Road, near the Fighting Cocks, an old tractor would tow us back to the Sunbeam works.

Sunbeam landed a contract for some test runs at Bournemouth about 1931, and with two other drivers I went down there to demonstrate a trolleybus on service, competing with vehicles from London United and another firm from the Leicester area. We won the competition and Sunbeam gained the contract to supply a hundred trolleybuses. When I came back to

Alan Butler poses by a Sunbeam Trolley Bus chasis on test. Note that the cab in which he had to drive was rather rudimentry, compared with the luxury provided for the engineers, and note the space provided at the stern for carrying ballast. As described in Alan Butler's account, these tests took place on the Wolverhampton-Sedgley-Dudley route. (Alan Butler's collection)

Wolverhampton I resumed my normal job and was classed as a Driver/Mechanic, based in Victoria Square. My job was to go out to any vehicle that broke down or failed, to try and get it going again, or to provide a substitute service with a single deck motor bus.

In 1936 I was promoted to Inspector. Each inspector had a section - mine was from Whitmore Reans way out to the north and west of the town. It involved a lot of footwork and you had to be as fit as a flea, but I enjoyed it. I had some wonderful drivers and conductors and we had no real problems.

Then the War started. I expected to go into the Navy but was told that my transport work was essential. Of course, you had to take other forms of defence work like Home Guard, Civil Defence, or Fire Service. Mr. Silvers sent for me and told me I would have to take responsibility for local defence business. I studied gas protection, bomb detection, and was already a member of the St. Johns Ambulance Brigade. I had to arrange fire practices for the Corporation Transport's Fire Brigade to turn out for fire drills and work out escape routes from our offices and cellars. I enjoyed doing all this immensely.

I also had to investigate a ticket fraud at the time. Revenue was dropping and we seemed to be selling an unusually high number of halfpenny tickets! I put my best suit on and sat at the back of a few buses to find out what was happening. I had a word with the Trade Union secretary and he discussed it with his branch committee, and everyone was keen to find a way of preventing conductors committing fraud. At the time we rented our ticket machines from Timco (Ticket Issuing Machine Company), and I found a way of reversing the dials on the top of the machine that would make the fraud impossible. We had to tell the men that it was being done as an experiment rather than to combat dishonesty, but it did the trick. The number of halfpenny tickets sold dropped and our revenue increased!

About 1942 the Chief Inspector was promoted to Traffic Superintendent and I was sent for and made Chief Inpsector. One wartime problem that I had to

deal with concerned finding a way of coping with all the extra traffic, and the extra services we had to provide to get people to and from their work. Everybody seemed to finish at the same time which made it extra difficult.

For example: we had to provide transport to Boulton and Paul out beyound Pendeford. According to the number of people we took down there for a quarter to eight in the morning, the company had to order buses to take them home - it was like a private hire arrangement as it was not one of our routes - but the works did not have to pay for it - the workers paid their own fares. Invariably more people finished at half past five than started at eight o' clock, and there was always a shortage of buses. The folks who couldn't get on the buses would walk along Claregate Lane blocking the road, so our buses had to trail along behind them at four miles per hour! We had a lot of trouble like that.

One night the Boulton and Paul workers threatened to throw me in the canal, but I said, "What if you throw me in the canal? Yo'll still have to walk home!" In the end they realised it was up to their company to order more buses. In turn we had to hire more buses to cope with the traffic. For example, we had about twenty Bournemouth buses operating in their colours for the rest of the War.

We also had to take on women conductors, and they were used on the Boulton and Paul service quite often. I remember one occcasion when one of the women conductors started having a baby upstairs. She was an unmarried woman and we did not even know she was expecting. The bus was full of blokes but they just left her there - lying on the floor. When I arrived I found the driver had fainted so I had to drive the bus myself. I drove right up to the gates at Boulton and Paul and demanded to be let through so we could take the girl straight to the works hospital. I'm glad to say she delivered the child safely.

Later in the forties, when Mr. Reid became ill, I became Traffic Superintendent, and I had that job until I retired in 1972.

Behind the Wheel

Vera Naylor

I have driven a car since I was seventeen - in fact, I've still got an "all groups" licence although I have never taken a driving test. You didn't need to take a test when I started driving. I was taught to drive by one of the Sunbeam test drivers. In those days every car chassis was thoroughly test driven before they put the bodies on, and the roads around Wolverhampton were full of Sunbeam testers! Otherwise there weren't many cars about then, and very few driven by women. If you stopped anywhere the first motorist to come past would stop to see if you were all right. Nowadays you could lie dead in the middle of the road for a fortnight and nobody would take any notice!

When the War came along married women had to register for War Work - if you had young chidren you were exempt, but if you had no children you had to do something. If you were working in a food shop you could usually carry on doing that, but it was no good me working in my husband's business because it was in the leather trade. Once registered I expected them to put me in a factory but I had never been one to stay in very much and I thought I would go mad if I ended up in a factory. I had to find something else to do before registration caught up with me.

I thought I would like to be a bus driver - there were one or two women driving buses in Wolverhampton at the time. My husband made enquiries and found that I would have to be a conductor first and he wouldn't allow me to do that - so that put an end to that idea.

One night I said to my husband, Tom, "There is an advert in the Express and Star for a lorry driver - I wish I could do that."
Tom said, "Well, couldn't you?"
So the very next morning I went round to J.V.Rushton's on the Birmingham Road, they were a firm that did anodising and plating, particularly of aircraft parts. I asked to see the manager.

"How long have you been driving lorries?" asked the manager.
"I haven't yet - I'm just hoping to start," I replied, pointing out that I had been driving since I was seventeen.
He said, "Well we have't had a women driver before so I don't know what the owner of the factory will think about it. I'll have to ask him first. If you come back this afternoon I'll tell you what he says."
I went back in the afternoon and was told, "The owner thinks it's good idea. You've got the job. Start on Monday morning."
When I got home I said to Tom, "I really don't know what I've done now - I've got the job as a lorry driver."

When I went along on the Monday morning I had a shock when I first saw the place because they had some lights that made everybody look purple. I thought they were all foreigners! The manager came along and said, "I've been thinking. Quite often we have small things to deliver and sometimes firms would like one or two components back right away, before the batch is completed. We've got a car here and I was wondering if you would like to drive that to start with before you go onto the lorries." I said

that that would be all right and was taken up to the garage - and there was a car identical to our own! It was a Standard 12. He called one of the other drivers over and said, "Take the car round the block and Mr. Cummings will come with you to see that everything is all right." Actually I think he wanted to know if I could really drive! - but of course I felt quite at home in that car.

I drove the car for a little while and then moved onto a Commer lorry. That was quite easy to drive and I eventually went on to a variety of vehicles. Once I had a very long one that carried the spars that went through aeroplane wings. My first trip in that lorry took me along the Birmingham Road to an island which existed at that time at the turning for Bilston. I thought to myself, "I've got to be very careful at this island - I've got to remember there's something at the back!", so I took a very wide sweep, but I took it too wide and realised that I wasn't going to get round. I stopped, and just as I had started to reverse I heard a huge cheer go up. I turned round to see another lorry driver who had recognised me and realised what I had done. Despite the cheering I backed up all right and went off to Bilston.

Another time I had to drive a big lorry loaned to us by the RAF. I liked driving that. You had to climb up the side - the driver was really high up and could see everything. People tell you not to drive anything too big but I would ten thousand times rather drive a big truck: you are up above everybody, you can see everything, people treat you with respect, and they are far easier to drive. I enjoyed every minute of it.

After I had been driving for a few days one of the men came to me and said, "Will you come up to the canteen?"
"When? Now?"
"Yes, we drivers are having a meeting. Its about you."
So I went along to the meeting, wondering what they were going to say.
The spokesman said, "Now, what Sunday work do you want?"
"Sundays? I haven't got to work Sundays have I? I've got a husband and a home to look after - I didn't think I was taking on Sunday work as well" (I just had not thought about it, and was quite shaken.)
"Well, no, you haven't got to work Sundays, but what we want to know is if you do want to, and when?"
"I don't want to work Sundays at all." At this everybody looked very relieved, and the spokesman said, "Well, OK, that's all right. I'll tell you what - we'll give you the choice of the day work - you can have first choice of the trips - but no Sunday work."
That really suited everybody, and I realised that they were getting double time on Sunday and were afraid that I was going to take the work off them! So I said, "Thanks very much - that suits me."

I used to start work at eight thirty but there was no fixed time for finishing. My last job of the day was to run the manager home to Dudley - he didn't care what he was taken home in, as long as he got a lift. and after doing that I could finish. My journeys often took me to places like Worcester or Shrewsbury and on the way back I would often fill the back of the lorry with servicemen. Everywhere you went there were servicemen hitching lifts and sometimes they were packed in like sardines but they didn't seem to mind as long as they got a lift. Whenever I arrived at a factory I had to go to the office and obtain a permit to give me access to their premises, and I've still got some of those passes today!

If I left the vehicle I had to immobilise it. Often I used to nip home for my lunch, so I would leave the lorry outside and take out the rotor arm. One day, after lunch, I couldn't find the rotor arm for a long while, so I decided to always leave it by the door. We had a bulldog at the time, but I never thought about him. One day I came back to the front door and there was my rotor arm in little bits all over the floor - he had chewed it all up! Luckily a nearby garage found me one straight away so I got away with it.

At the end of the War there was suddenly notification that people could leave their War jobs if they wanted to do so and I had to give up lorry driving and help my husband in the shop. I was glad that I had done it - I still felt that I would have gone mad if I had sat in a factory all day.

R.B.Tudor's coal yard at the Albion Wharf, Oldbury about 1949. The horse drawn narrowboats tied up at the wharf, and the lorries are nicely lettered in the name of the company. The boats are being unloaded onto the wharf and the sacks are being put onto the lorry, as described by Harry Tonks. The nearest boat is the Stroud, the far one is the Charity. Joe Haines is on the lorry on the left, watched by Robert Tudor almost hidden by the lorry on the right, driven by Les Rogers with Joe Ceney looking out of the window. All lorries are Fords. The photo (by Sidney Darby) is taken from the roof of the office and shows the stables on the extreme left and the "new" garage built in the early 1940s. The same view in 1989 would reveal that the arm of the canal serving the wharf has now been filled in and the yard moved beyond the fence in the background. Once employing thirty men and running a fleet of boats and coal lorries the company is now left with about ten percent of its former business. (Robert Tudor's collection)

Carrying Coal on the Cut

Harry Tonks

My stepfather worked on the canals and when I was twelve I used to go with him on Saturday afternoons to pull the boat from Sandwell Colliery to Albion. (He worked for R.B.Tudor, who were coal merchants working from a wharf at Albion.) We had to pull the empty boat up through the three locks at Spon Lane and come back loaded. At the wharf the boat was unloaded and the coal was put in bags for delivery around the houses.

I left school about 1940, at the age of fourteen, and wanted to work on the canal but there wasn't a job available straight away. I worked briefly at a foundry, but a chap was given the sack at Tudor's, and I was given his job. Funnily enough he was taken back on sometime later and I ended up working with him.

R.B.Tudor expanded and we started to go to Cannock Chase for the coal. Starting from the wharf we had to go down the eight locks and out through Toll End, Wednesbury, Darlaston, Pleck and to Walsall, where there were eight more locks, then through Bloxwich, Pelsall, and Norton Canes to the Chase, or to the Hednesford Arm, which we called "The Bumper". Tudors had first used their delivery horse to pull a canal boat when not out on deliveries, but these trips to Cannock Chase took a day and a half there and back with a horse drawn boat. They had to buy four horses, stabled at the wharf, and they had to hire boats from Jimmy Yates at Norton Canes.

Two of us worked the horse drawn boats, one on the boat and the other leading the horse. As a young chap I preferred being on the boat, as it seemed a fair way to walk when you were leading a horse to Hednesford. Once a horse got used to the job, and knew the way himself, we would both travel on the boat, and this was called "backering". Having gone up one day, and come back the next, we then had to shovel the coal out of the boat and onto the wharf - leaving the jaggers to put it in bags and weigh it. The coal was in four piles in the boat - the stern, the stern middle, fore middle and fore end.

In the early fifties we started using a motor boat. The round trip could now be done in fifteen or sixteen hours, if you had a good road there and back. We would leave the wharf at 1.00.am and be back by the evening, five days a week. Later the motor boat towed two butty boats and the trip was only made three times a week, but if you went via Wolverhampton, in order to work less locks, the trip could take twenty hours.

We used to collect coal from Harrison's at Brownhills, from the Conduit Colliery at Norton, the Coppice Colliery (The Fair Lady), Cannock and Leacroft, Hawkins of Cheslyn Hay, East Cannock and Cannock & Rugeley. Hawkins was down thirteen locks but we used to leave an empty boat at the top and pick up a loaded one - they had two fellows of their own who worked the boats up and down the locks. At some of the pits, like East Cannock and Brownhills, for example, the coal was loaded directly from the washerie. Sometimes at East Cannock they loaded three boats at once - one with clear coal, one with slack, and one with D&S Nuts or the big Bakers Nuts that Ratcliffe's used to like. At other places, like Mid Cannock, they loaded us from lorries and I didn't think there was any future in that. I think Mid Cannock was the first to close, in the mid fifties, and the others gradually dwindled away.

I was always impressed by the "Hampton Boats", big boats that worked a level stretch between Wolverhampton and the Cannock Coalfield. John Toole had the two biggest; "Jill" and "Jeremy". They were about ninety feet long and wider than other boats, so they couldn't work a lock. A lot of the Wolverhampton area coal merchants had big boats; Jones & Powell of Lanesfield, Wulfruna and Sammy Jones, and Proberts at Millfields. They posed quite a problem at the stop places where the loads had to be gauged and they worked out how much travelling money had to be paid. The coal wharves had to pay a higher rate than the industrial users.

If I go back to the War years, and the days of the horse boats, it is staggering to think how much traffic was using the canal. A lot of power station traffic was carried by boat and there was much traffic between gas works and chemical plants. In the winter the canals were closed from six till six by locking up the locks and dropping the stop planks. This was done in case the canal was bombed at night and the bank was breached. It removed the threat of the entire canal being emptied and the reulting floods. But it made the canal even busier by day!

Sometimes when we reached the Walsall locks we would find twenty boats waiting ahead of us. If one of Ernest Thomas's boats from Walsall came down while you were waiting the entire queue would be brought to a standstill for half an hour. There were distance stumps you had to reach to claim your lock. If your horse had got his head to the stump you were supposed to have first entry to the lock, but once or twice there were scraps over it.

I used to know the people who lived on the boats, and most of the lock-keepers, and I still see quite a few of them now. Our boats were just ordinary wooden butty boats - we bought six of them from King Brothers of Aston Cross. They could carry about thirty five tons, and I still remember their names to this day: Forward, Success, Endeavour, Charity, Faith, and Stroud. Of course we also grew attached to our horses.

We had a Belgian horse called Jim. He would set out first thing in the morning, and his pace would still be the same last thing at night - he never slowed down. But if he broke the line he'd run off and you couldn't catch him! One day he broke the line at Bromford Bridge, ran off and took half the line with him. My mate went after him and jumped on a passing lorry, but even at 30mph they still couldn't catch him. In West Bromwich he was hit by a lorry and was knocked down. The vet was called but no sooner had he touched him than the horse was up and ready to go again - he was perfectly all right! We sold Jim when we bought the motor boat but Jack was kept to do the local trips to Sandwell Colliery. They were good looking black horses - like funeral horses.

I had never had anything to do with motors but I got used to the motor boat, and eventually worked it by myself. But I never fancied driving a lorry and delivering coal. Of course we did have occasional problems with the motor boat - particularly the propeller getting clogged up. One day at Golds Hill a whole fire hose got wrapped round the propeller and I had to get in the cut to unravel it. We were usually paid so much a trip, or "voyage" as we called it. I was paid quite a lot extra working the motor boat myself.

As the collieries closed, or the traffic was transferred to the road, there was less to do, and I found myself helping out on the wharf or doing local trips where we used the boats to deliver coal rather than bring it in. For example I took coal to Gibbons at Tividale, shovelled the coal into 5cwt. barrows and wheeled it out to them. (They paid me thirty bob extra to do that.) And I'd fetch their ash away and take it down the tip.

I left Tudor's in 1965 and did a couple of other jobs. I never thought I would be able to work inside, yet I worked for Grovewood Kitchen Furniture for fifteen years. I really enjoyed being outside on the canal, I liked always travelling somewhere and doing the different jobs. Occasionally we took coal down to Walter Somers in Halesowen, via the Netherton Tunnel, and I legged the boat through Gorsty Hill Tunnel, but I've never been through the Dudley tunnel. There's no commercial traffic on the canal today - it's all pleasure boats, but I still spend most of my time walking the canals and helping people on the boats wherever I can.

7

SERVING THE PUBLIC

*In area once dominated by manufacturing and heavy indus-
try, it easy to lose sight of the work done in the "service" area;
the public services and local government, retailing, the
maintenance and repair of our possessions, entertainment
etc. These four chaps worked for the Health Department of
Bilston Borough Council in the 1950s providing a public
service of a very specialised kind - they were the "Fumigation
Squad" in charge of disinfestation of council tenants' homes.*

Delivering the Mail

Margaret Davies

Just after the last War I went to the Post because
I noticed that they were advertising for women. Before
they would give you the job you had to take an exam,
but, as well as passing that, I had to sign a contract
promising to surrender my job if it was wanted by a
man. It seemed fair to me because I knew men would
be needing jobs, but I also knew that it was a job that
sometimes men did not want to do, although I couldn't
understand why. At first I was sent out with another
postman who showed me the round, but after that I
was on my own.

My round was on the Scotlands. I had to start at
Leason Lane and end up at the bottom of Tennyson
Road. I had to leave home to catch the bus at five
o'clock in the morning to make sure I was at the
Wolverhampton sorting Office by six. We had to do

our own sorting and plan our route and very often we
were on the bus out of town again by seven. We got
to know all the bus crews that we saw regularly. Later
we would get back to the Office for a break and then
sort again for a second delivery. Sometimes there were
two rounds in one where we would use a bike because
we would be doing collections as well.

We used to finish about one o'clock, although sometimes we had to deliver circulars or pools coupons in
the afternoon as overtime. I liked to be home by the
time the children came home from school. We had
three children and my mother could cover for me while
I was at work, especially during the school holidays -
or my husband might be at home because he worked
shifts on the railway. One problem was that we had
to work on Christmas Day and take the time off at
some other time.

It was hard work; they were big rounds and we
carried heavy loads and parcels which I reckon go on
the van nowadays. And we had some terrible winters

at that time. I remember doing one round near Bantock Park and I had to cross the park to empty a box despite the fact that the park was under at least a foot of snow. At Christmas we seemed to work very long hours even though the Office took on a lot of help.

But what I really liked about the job was the people I met. I met some lovely people on the Scotlands. I know they were very poor, but they were very nice, and always used to share a joke with me. They used to say to me, "We can set our clocks by you - you're never late - and we always know when your not here, because if someone else does the round they call at a different time." Some of the old people would say, "Read this one to me - it's from my son in Australia." For invalides we often fetched prescriptions on our way to and from the Office.

We had a choice of uniform - either a skirt and jacket or trousers and jacket - made from a very thick serge, edged with red. The shoes were made of very hard leather and were terrible to wear. I've had more blisters on my heels than you've had letters, but you needed them in the bad winters. As we went into work an Inspector would be there to inspect your uniform and make sure you were clean and tidy.

One day I had just started out up Leason Lane, and I was really loaded with parcels tied to my bag. I was going up Wordsworth Road with a big parcel for one particular house, where the light was on and I could hear the wireless going. When nobody answered the door I assumed they were in the kitchen so I went round the back. I couldn't rouse anybody but I was determined not to carry the parcel any further so I thought I'd put it in the toilet. I opened the toilet door only to find a man sitting there, so I just threw the parcel in and ran off. I felt so embarassed I couldn't look at the house for a few mornings!

On another occasion I had to go from one house to the next via a very long wall so I thought I would save myself going all the way round and simply climb over the wall. I just had one leg over the wall when my bag swung over and pulled me over. As I landed on the floor a man came out of the house and said, "What are you doing there?"
"I'm just getting up," I replied, "I fell over the wall." He looked at me and said, "Would you mind using the path another time? That's what paths are made for."

Once they put me on a new round that took me to New Cross and I delivered a load of letters before I saw the correct letter box and had to ask the people to come and collect their mail from where I had put it. I discovered that I had posted their letters in the fowl pen!

At first it was strange working with a lot of men. Some of them were a bit nasty and seemed to think their jobs were in jeopardy - as if their jobs were going to be taken by women. They said, "You shouldn't be here," and "A woman's place is in the home." We took no notice of them because we needed the money and felt we were willing to work for it - and we had signed the contract to say that a man could have our job if he wanted it. After they got used to us they were really helpful - they were nice fellows really!

There was one Inspector who was a really nice man, Mr.Reynolds. He could get anything done because of his attitude towards you. He wasn't a person to say, "You've gotta do this." He would come along and say, "I'm in a bit of a jam today, there are so many people

off, do you think you could do an extra half round?" We would always say, "Yes," and during those Flu epidemics we would do one round, come back, and do another, just to help him out! It was a lovely time of my life because of the people I met and, because I always took biscuits with me, I was never bitten by the dogs. And I enjoyed seeing the different ways people lived.

They were the best days of my life.

Margaret Davies, on the right, and her friend Gwen Grayson, photographed among the sorting racks at GPO sorting office in Wolverhampton in the late 1940's. Gwen always took a supply of dog biscuits with her on her round to pacify any unfriendly dogs! (Margaret Davies's collection)

George Bytheway while marking up the newspapers for delivery from his shop in Wolverhampton Street, Dudley. (Donald Blytheways's collection)

George Bytheway's shop in Wolverhampton Street, Dudley, 1911. Note the slim barber's pole by the door — George was still barbering, while selling books, making umbrellas, and building up the business as a stationer and newsagent. Donald's mother and sister stand in the shop doorway. The display in the right hand window includes handbills for the Public Hall, where Irving Bosco had been showing films since January 1910, and the Criterion which started showing films regularly in 1911. (Donald Bytheway's collection)

Selling the News

Donald Bytheway

My newsagents shop in Wolverhampton Street, Dudley, has a story going back to the days before the First World War. It all goes back to the time when my father, George, at the age of fourteen, was sent away to Liverpool to an uncle in the hairdressing. He returned, and when he was seventeen he opened a hairdressing shop at the top of Himley Road. A few years later an uncle from Liverpool, a vicar, told him to get nearer the town, so he moved to the present address, where I eventually practiced the business.

Although my father had started out as a hairdresser he found that hairdressing fell off and he started selling papers to make up. Shaving really disappeared after the First War because the men who had been soldiers in the trenches were used to shaving themselves, but he still did a little shaving and barbering until the Second World War. In his early days he also used to make umbrellas to earn a living.

In the early days there were no wholesale people in Dudley for the newsagents and the papers came by train to Dudley station. My father had to be down at Dudley station at five o' clock in the morning to

collect them. He built a special barrow and called it the "skeleton barrow" - just two long bars and a bar or two across and a bar at the front, so that there was no weight in it. The parcels of papers were piled onto it and then wheeled up Castle Hill and right up to the shop. He also carried parcels for Burgins to give to old lady Burgin, and parcels for Cartwright, the newsagent at Sedgley. The latter were carried as far as Parson Street where the trams from Wolverhampton terminated. They were put on a tram and the conductor had to throw them off right outside Cartwright's shop as they passed through Sedgley!

Sometimes the train, coming up from Tipton, couldn't make it into Dudley station, the engine would slip as it came under the Tipton Road bridge, and my father, and others, would have to get down on the track and go and unload the parcels direct from the train. The weather could also delay the papers in winter. But the customers didn't care about the weather. They paid for their papers and expected to get them before seven o'clock in the morning. Even in thick fog they used to grumble at us.

86

As youngsters my sister and I had to deliver the papers. I well remember one morning as I went down Himley Road with the papers in a terrible thick fog one fellow came out saying, "If yo' can't bring it earlier than this - don't bring it any more!" That's how they treated you. In 1923 H.R.Taylor established a wholesaling business in Dudley in Stone Street, followed right away by W.H.Smith in Castle Street. That cut out the trips to the station, but papers could still arrive late.

I came into the business when I left school in the early thirties. It was a real newsagency then - you had to make your living out of selling newspapers, sweets and cigarettes. Things changed after the Second World War but I carried on in the business until I retired in 1983 when my wife was taken ill.

In the twenties and thirties the newsagents had a Federation, which was a sort of Trade Union. They had a little bit of power in those days and if someone wanted to start selling papers they had to apply to the Federation. My father was the secretary and he had to put the applications before a committee. If you wanted to open a newsagency and there was already one just down the road, the latter would be consulted about how well he served the area etc. If he said that the area was already well served the applicants would always give the tale that they had been in business for a while and were always being asked for papers!

An unemployed fellow who used to come into or shop was sent by my father to watch the applicant's business and fetch a book and pencil out and make a note of how many people walked up and down the street, and how many went into the shop and all that sort of thing. He would come back and give my father the report, and my father would give him a bob or two for doing it - and the Federation could then say there was no room for another newsagency there. In most cases the wholesalers would accept it and not supply the applicant with papers, but sometimes it would go the other road and a new shop would be opened.

After the War my father was still the secretary of the Federation in an unpaid capacity until he went into hospital. Later the post became a paid job, not part of somebody's beliefs and principles as it had been with my father. Then such "restrictive practices" became illegal and the Federation lost its power. The wholesalers were then prepared to put papers wherever they could - and that's how it all changed. Selling papers today isn't a trade; it's a sideline!

Of course we did sell more than just papers. In the old days you could buy anything at our shop. We used to sell toys until Woolworths done the toy trade in. We used to sell tuppenny bottles of cough spirit and tuppenny bottles of iodine and rolls of bandages, but the National Health done all that in! But newspapers were seventyfive percent of our trade from the pre-War days until the 1950s. Yet, by the time I retired, I couldn't sell a paper over the counter of my shop unless it had been ordered. We used to sell so many periodicals as well - women's magazines, Peck's Paper, Boy's Cinema, Boy's Own, Girl's Own, Magnets, Gems, Red Letters, Secrets, Red Star Weeklies,... hundreds of them, all at tuppence a time.

We used to have five lads delivering for us, even then the family often had to help out. Our children, like me, were put to the grindstone! Two of the lads told me, at different times, that the last thing they would ever want to do was to be a newsagent. We had to work seven days a week and our only holidays were Christmas Day, Boxing Day and Good Friday. Two of the lads also told me that their mothers had said that we got the papers for nothing - the price was all profit! To know and understand a newsagent's life of those days you would have to have been one.

Sometimes we had customers who left the shop without paying. My father, who was a real Blackcountryman, used to have a Staffordshire Bull Terrier named Gyp. My father would send Gyp after such customers. He'd be off down the road after them, and they used to put the money in his mouth and Gyp would bring it back and give it to my father.

A newsagent isn't allowed to be ill - you still have to be out delivering papers when often you should be in bed - and it's not as if the customers were grateful. My father always used to remind us of the time when papers went up from a halfpence to a penny during the First World War. One customer came into the shop to scream in protest, "Now I can only have my Daily Mail on a Monday, a Wednesday and a Saturday!" I can remember one newsagent at Dudley Port. He retired from the trade donkeys years ago and he said to my father, after his retirement, "George, I feel as if I've been let out of jail!"

Winning the War

Lucy Price (Then Lucy Griffiths)

At fourteen and a half years of age I left school. I should have stayed on but I had decided I wanted to work in a shop and my enthusiasm for shop work was so strong it was decided that I should leave school there and then. For the first six months of my working life I worked as a shop assistant at the "Valeting Service" in Dudley's Fountain Arcade.

It was just a small shop with a small area partitioned off where we had our morning and afternoon cup of tea. It was a most interesting place to work and there was just myself and the manageress, who was very kind. We didn't ever stand about though because as people brought in their skirts and coats for cleaning, we had to sew into each garment a number. Each number had to be in a different colour, depending on what job had to be done. I only stayed in the job for six months because I decided I would like to broaden my outlook. The fact was I felt very shy, as many young people were in those days, and I thought if I went to work in a bigger shop, with more people and more going on, that perhaps I would overcome my shyness.

I had an interview with the Manageress of Grey's in Dudley's High Street, and when I went to work there I found it was very different to the "Valeting Service". Of course, it was quite a big shop, and most interesting. The manageress said she was interested in me and wanted me to learn as much as I could, so I worked on most of the counters during my time there.

The discipline was extremely stern, and the "floor walkers", as I believe we called them, were particu-

A First Hand was really an assistant manager, and, of course, had to take over in the manager's absence. While at Penn Road I began studying by correspondence course for the examinations available through the Cooperative Union. The Co-op did not give you time off to study - it had to be done in your own time. For the first two years I paid for all my own studies, but eventually the Education Committee got to know about it and they decided to pay for my courses. Meanwhile I was transfered to No.1. Branch in Newhampton Road and after about twelve months I was made a manager at the Coseley Branch. After that I worked at a number of stores; Bushbury, Stubby Lane, No.53 at Parkfields, and Deans Road.

While managing these stores I started to do a little teaching and found myself given the job of Education Secretary. I had to take the minutes at the meetings of the Education Committee, formed of ordinary Society members and representatives of the Board of Management, running all the educational side of the Society's affairs. We looked after the Women's Guilds, of which there were five. We organised courses and speakers for them, sometimes liasing with the WEA, the Workers Educational Association. We also looked after the youth groups. We had paid youth leaders and I had to visit them regularly to see that everything was running correctly. All this had to be done in my spare time, but it was very different to running the shop so it was a nice change. My efforts were partly paid - I think I was given £2 a month for being Education Secretary! And I was rewarded with time off once a year to attend the annual Education Convention.

We were happy doing our work in the shops and we did seem to work together as a team. If you don't do that it soon shows and you start losing trade. There were problems to face like pilfering and having to balance the books to the nearest penny, but I did enjoy the work. I also found the teaching very interesting. It was very difficult at first but the more you got into it, the more you got to know how to tackle things. If you tackled it wrongly, you got the wrong results - the class went to sleep! With book-keeping I know I made a horrible mess of it the first year, because I had learnt it from a textbook and tried to teach it the same way but it didn't work. The second year we were all right and the third year we were laughing. We obtained the largest number of book-keeping passes in the country!

Usually I was engaged in training Co-op employees but it extended after a while because I was doing it under the auspices of Wulfrun College - they paid my salary. Once we were joined by some Beatties students for Business Organisation, but they did not like coming onto Co-op premises so we had to use school premises.

larly stern. Although I was very much in awe of Mrs. Burton, the manageress, she combined sterness with kindness. If she thought someone was upset or worried she would have that person in her office for a talk and be as much help as she could. The customers came first and we always had to be courteous and helpful. We worked on a commission basis depending on whether we were first, second, third or fourth sales. The "First Sales" was the buyer for the department, and as I was the youngest, I was the "Fourth Sales". I used to feel a bit upset at not being able to serve a customer unless the first, second and third sales were serving, but if they were occupied and I had the chance to serve I put everything into it. I progressed from fourth to second sales.

One Christmas I was "in charge" of a little department of my own; the Stationery Department, and I loved it. I served customers as happily and busily as I could. In those days life was pleasant despite a terrible War. I was there from 1939 to 1941 and young men were going to war and to munitions work but people were kind to each other and helpful. For a time I worked in the millinery department. There were piles and piles of hats, all stacked up and we had to continually brush these hats. If I was serving a customer and it looked as if she wasn't going to make a purchase and I could see Mrs. Burton coming I would keep that customer talking, because it wasn't the thing to lose a sale and the manageress would look very disapproving if you did lose the sale. I loved the selling, but I didn't think much of brushing hats.

I later went to Hill's and Steele's in Market Place, and this was a very different store. I liked it better because the shop was more central and was therefore more busy. I worked in the Food Department where we had queues for everything, and I was really in my element. At one time they moved me to window dressing, which would have been a good job, but the thing that I loved was serving customers. I cried so much the manager decided it would be better to put me back behind the counter. I loved serving the queues of customers and getting to know them. I remember a bus conductress who used to work shifts. I always "saved" her a tin of salmon. She used to come in through the main doors with her little boy and I would say, "I've got a tin of salmon for you!" She always looked so pleased - after all, a tin of salmon was a luxury in those days.

I also remember that we had three bells at the end of the day when the shop closed. The first bell was for manning the doors while customers left the shop. The second bell was for putting out the fire buckets, and the third bell was for "cashing up". I worked as many hours as I could, including stock-taking every other Sunday. I also did "fire-watching" in turns. Each evening two girls would come in about eight o' clock and stay until work next day. We had a kind and fatherly night watchman who told us to stay in the staffroom while he would go down into the store to check everything.

Although I had been told I would be promoted to floor walker, I felt I wanted to help the War Effort. I was then seventeen but my parents did not want me to join the forces so I felt as if I should go and work on munitions. I went to work at Ewarts at Burnt Tree but after twelve months about a hundred of us became redundant and so I went to work at Accles and Pollack in Oldbury. That also filled two happy years of my life. The people working there came from all over England, and we all got on very well together. I had to learn to read a vernier and a "mike".

I worked for a year on lathes - one week nights, one week days, on eleven hour shifts. But I could not sleep in the day and on my doctor's advice I worked the day shifts only. As a result I was taken off the lathes and put on drilling machines. There were only four of us women working on the drillers and I was the only single girl. Once I went on strike because I felt the married women were being favoured. Ray, our chargehand, thought it was all a big joke until he realised I was in real earnest. From then on he was more considerate of how he set the work out. Certainly we all worked hard and earnt our money. The break times were great. We had music played to us from our own records put on by the security man at the gates. I used to ask for Joe Loss and "In the Mood". They were happy days. Although the news was grim and we were all very concerned about what was going to happen, we were all sure of one thing: we were going to win the War!

A Job for Life

Ken Grainger

I started work in 1938 with the Rotherham Cooperative Society at a little grocery shop in the village of Dinnington. In those days it was the thing if you joined the Co-op. If you managed to get a job with them you were there for life. My father was a miner and he felt it was most important that you had a job for life. In fact he paid £150 for me to be able to leave shool early, because I should have stayed until I was sixteen, so that I could start work at the Co-op.

I started as a Flour Boy - thats what we were called in those days. My job was to weigh up the flour. People used to bake their own bread and, consequently, we used to sell eighty sacks of flour a week. I had to weigh out the flour, do all the running about, and occasionally go out delivering odds and ends.

After about eighteen months I was promoted to behind the counter. My word, you were somebody in those days when you found yourself behind a counter actually serving. I was there when the War came along and was then transfered to another shop to take the place of a man who had been called up. I was there for three years until I was called up and went into the RAF. Eventually I came to Cosford to be trained as a flight mechanic and that is how I met Audrey, who was working for the Wolverhampton Cooperative Society. I came out of the forces in 1947 and we got married.

We went back to Dinnington but Audrey maintained contact with the Wolverhampton people, and Mr. Briggs, the Drapery Manager suggested that we return to Wolverhampton as promotion was so slow up there. Thus one year later I took a First Hand's job with Wolverhampton Cooperative Society. I found that I had come to one of the first shops in the country to be opened on the self-service principle, and that was at Penn Road.

One reason that being a grocery branch manager was interesting was that all the branches were different - reflecting the type of people who came in. You gradually got to know them and learnt to talk in the way that they expected you to talk. If you were in an ordinary store and talked posh they would just laugh you straight out of the store! But managers had no pretensions - we had to do everything from sweeping the floors to dressing and cleaning the windows. In fact it was my job to sweep the snow away as none of the girls would do it.

Fellow managers would help each other out and once a year we all got together for a trip. Usually we went to a CWS factory somewhere - to see how they canned peas and that sort of thing. It was educational but interesting, but for some it was also quite a boozy trip! Although there was much to enjoy in my "job for life" there was a time when I became disillusioned. After the Walsall Society took us over all the educational side of my work disappeared because they had their own Education Department. I left and became an Accounts Office Manager for Delta Water Fittings, turning my back on the Co-op after all.

Dressing the Windows

Audrey Grainger

My first acquaintance with the Wolverhampton Cooperative Society's store in Lichfield Street, Wolverhampton, was during my childhood. I used to go there with my mother to buy my shoes and school uniform. At the time the whole of the Co-op was just on the ground floor and the general offices were at the back of the shop. It was a very old-fashioned place.

By 1941 I had just completed two years full time at the Art School and the Headmaster was asking me what I wanted to do. I told him that I wanted to be a window dresser, because my father had been one. The Head asked me where I wanted to work. I knew that the Co-op was being altered - being made much bigger, with lots of windows, so I felt that would be a better opportunity than an established place like Beatties which already had everything. He arranged an inter-

view for me, and on a Wednesday afternoon I set off to Lichfield Street.

As it happened the windows of the Co-op had been dressed by anyone up until that time. However, Mr.Briggs, the Drapery Manager, had thought there ought to be a "Display Department". They had already appointed a girl from Beatties and were looking for further staff. I was interviewed in the General Manager's new office, a place that seemed like a palace to me. It was lined with panels of light oak and contained a enormous nine foot by nine foot leather topped desk. Behind this desk was the Secretary & General Manager and the Assistant Secretary & General Manager, and the Drapery Manager. At the end of the interview they said that they were still thinking about setting up the Display Department, but probably not until later. They would let me know.

I went back to the Art School thinking I had wasted my time but on my return the Headmaster sent for me and told me that they had already rung through and wanted me to start the next day! I was sixteen years old and starting work was quite a shock. I was used to finishing at the Art School at four thirty but the Co-op used to work until seven on Monday and Wednesday, until six on Tuesday, and until eight on Friday and Saturday. (Half-day on Thurday finished at one.) These hours were reduced by the effects of Wartime until we closed at five every night.

I was junior to the girl who had come to set up the department and we were given a tiny little Display Stock Room down in the basement. (Half the basement was the Hardware Department and a cafe/restaurant occupied the rest of the space. However, just after I started they opened up the first floor. Work had started on this in 1939 and, although the War was on, they were allowed to finish off a certain ammount of the work. They also completed part of the second floor and much of the frontage was refurbished. To us it was very exciting to move up onto a new floor. Fashions were up there and it all seemed so modern. In the end they decided to put our little Display Department on the third floor at the front - in the old rooms of the original building - but, at last, we had several rooms, one of which could be made into a studio.

Also on the third floor was a caretaker's flat. Mr.

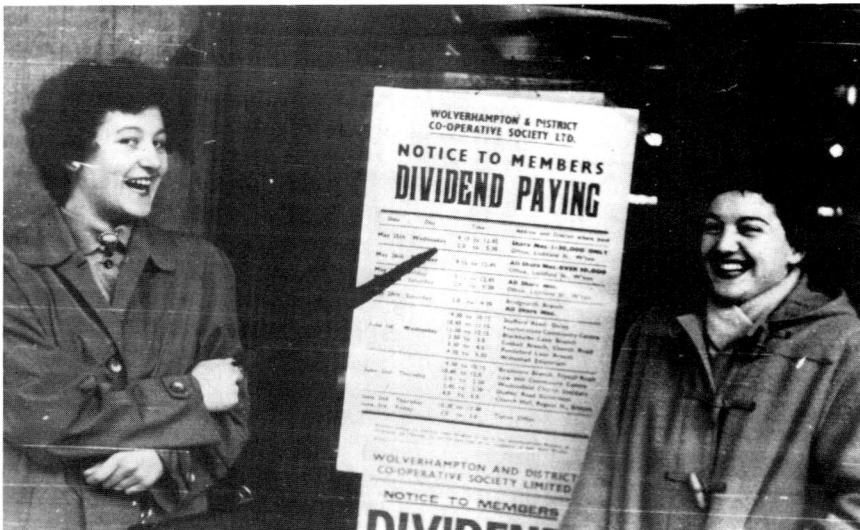

Maisie Kearns (left) and Marjorie Bowman (right) of Wolverhampton Cooperative Society anticipate the stress of Dividend week, May 1955. (Marjorie Bowman's collection)

and Mrs. Jordan lived there and he developed a lovely little garden on the roof. He put window boxes all along our canopy in Lichfield Street and provided the store with hanging baskets. Together with the new stone facing applied to our frontage our store looked very smart. New staircases and lifts also had to be provided. While these were being built I had to go up the internal fire escape, across the flat roof outside, across a plank over a drop that went right down to the basement, and climb through a dormer window to get into our Display Department.

Like all other staff I had to do fire-watching duties. We stayed overnight in the old rooms at the top of the building - one room for the girls and one room for the men. Nobody used to sleep very much because it was all so much fun. We did not appreciate the seriousness of it all.

The girl from Beatties that I was working for married a Dutchman and left the Society and I was offered the job of Senior Display Person at the age of eighteen. I was given two assistants who had just left school. We felt we were very "way out" compared with the rest of the staff because we wore slacks and blouses to dress the windows. When I started at the store the men wore black pin striped trousers and black coats. The girls wore black dresses with white collars, and we all had to call each other by our surnames. The atmosphere was strict but fair.

Being eighteen I had to register for War work. I did not want to go in the forces, nor was I very keen on munitions work. Mr. Briggs suggested that if I transferred to a Food Department I would be in a Reserved Occupation. "I'll have a word with the dairy," he said. Then I was asked if I would consider doing a milk round? I said that I would, thinking that it would be an easy little job - driving a van round and plonking milk on the steps. Mr. Briggs unfolded his plan a little further, "You will start very early in the morning, but you finish by lunchtime - and then you could come back to the shop in the afternoons and dress the windows to keep your hand in!" It all sounded fine to me.

When I started delivering milk it turned out to be a bit of an eye-opener because it was a much heavier job than I had expected. We had to load our own vans and the metal crates, loaded three at a time, were very dirty and heavy. And I hadn't thought about the weather - it was tougher than expected! But at least I was learning to drive, which was a bonus, and I had to be a mate while I did so. I had to acquire a thick leather coat for the winter, but I had to go to a second hand shop because rationing made it so difficult to have the coupons for such things.

At the dairy I had to work seven days a week - you never had the one day off a week that you were supposed to have. But we did have Christmas Day off! From Monday to Thursday I could finish at one o'clock and rush back to the store to dress windows, but Friday and Saturday I spent collecting the money. I did that for two and a half years.

My milkround was in Whitmore Reans. Milk was rationed of course - two pints per person per week and two and a half for adults in summer, children up to ten had three and a half pints a week, babies a pint a day and expectant mothers a pint a day. I used to get to know when all the mothers were pregnant because they had to give me the special chit to get extra milk, saying, "Don't tell anyone I'm pregnant and

please leave the milk round the back so that no one will know."

A window cleaner was always asking me to let him drive my van. I always refused, but one day I came back from some houses and my van had gone! I ran round the corner and found that he had driven it into a wall. I had to pretend that I had crashed it rather than admit to the dairy that someone else had driven my van.

After the War Mr. Briggs was keen to build up the Display Department and get the other managers interested in our work so that we could work for the whole store. Eventually we convinced everybody and we took responsibility for the entire store and became a big department. We took to decorating the store for Christmas as a complete entity. Later we designed and built our first Christmas grotto. One year we devoted an entire window to the Nativity scene - no goods on show at all - and it was a huge success. Someone wrote to the Express and Star suggesting that a Nativity scene should in future be put by the Christmas tree in St. Peters' Gardens.

We also organised fashion shows. We used the hall above Central Grocery in Stafford Street and built our own catwalk. In 1947 the New Look arrived and I designed a backdrop with a figure in 1847 dress on the left and a nude figure on the right with a big question mark round it. Six mannequins from Balloon Street, Manchester, came down and opened the show with a costume from each decade since 1847 until we announced the New Look. But when the Board of Management heard about the nude they went beserk. Once again Mr. Briggs came to my rescue and backed my plans. Later on we moved these shows to the Civic Hall, we used our own girls as models and I compered the shows.

I greatly enjoyed all these activities as well as going on buying trips and the annual British Display Association conferences. These later became international which was even more exciting. We became a bigger section as more artists joined us and eventually the store appointed a Publicity Manager so we went into his section - advertising, publicity and display all became one.

We were a happy shop. We enjoyed trips, dances, dinners and drama groups together and I think we were a very close staff. But all good things come to an end. The CWS took over the Society for a couple of years and the shop was turned into CWS Homemaker - doing away with everything except furniture, carpets and household goods. Things were no longer "displayed" - they were just "put in the window". I retired after working forty three years for the Co-op.

Left to right: Marjorie Bowman, Eileen Jones and Maisie Kearns in the cashiers' central office of Wolverhampton Cooperative Society's Lichfield Street store on 3rd December 1955. Marjorie stands by her beloved "wind machine" connected by tube to every counter in the store. (Marjorie Bowman's collection.)

The Wind Machine

Marjorie Bowman

When I finished school my mother decided that the Co-op was a good place for me to work. I didn't question why. That was 1944. I continued not to ask any questions and stayed there until 1967. Having stayed only twenty three years I never got the gold watch!

It was very easy to get the job. There was plenty of work while the War was on. The men were away fighting and the girls were going into factories like mad because thats where the money was, but there was no money in working for the Co-op.

I simply started in a very lowly way - in the Sorting Office, sorting those checks that were given when you bought goods over the counter and they tore off a perforated check about as big as a double stamp. We sorted those from morn till night. We young things worked long hours - forty four hours a week for 17/6, later rising to a pound. It was like being back at school, except that we had to sit down a lot, which I wasn't used to. We each had to do a week's duty on the lift because the store had no permanent lift man, and this duty came round about once every twelve weeks. One of my early memories is the notice that used to be stuck under every light switch: "When this switch is DOWN our electricity bill is UP".

I used to spend my lunch hours in the Cash Office which is where all the money came in from the counters all over the store. Money was carried to the office by the suction method in tubes, in a system built by the Dart Cash Carrier Company of Stoke-on-Trent. When the men from Stoke came to repair the system I felt they had come from another world - Stoke seemed so far away!

I helped one of the two girls that worked in that office while the other was at lunch. I came to like her in the way that you like teachers at school because she was a nice woman, and she taught me the job. After five years, when a vacancy occurred, I was in there like a shot, and eventually I took over her job. Thus for about ten years I was the "Cashier in charge". It didn't seem quite such an important job once I was doing it.

From the windows of the store in Lichfield Street it was possible to watch important people coming to the Vic or The Grand Theatre. I used to take a camera to work! I saw Winston Churchill, Joan Greenwood and Margaret Lockwood. I'm afraid Churchill didn't come into the Co-op even although we did sell cigars. (In fact we had a tobacco kiosk right on the front of the store, and it did quite well.)

At one time they wanted a new name for the Co-op store in Lichfield Street, and asked the staff to come up with a good name. I thought of "Unity", put it down on my card, and won. I won ten shillings (50p), in the form of a voucher that had to be spent in the store. I don't think the name was ever used but I was able to buy a suitcase with the prize.

We were always told we were the "poor relations" to Beatties. The staff there were very much a "cut above" us at the Co-op even though we were doing the same work. But we didn't let that worry us - we thought we had a bit more fun. We had lovely Christmas Parties where we all did turns, and we had a lovely Sports Ground in the Compton Road behind some allotments. Going down there on our bikes was like going to the country. The Co-op owned it - and I don't think Beatties had a Sports Ground! We had a Ladies Cricket Team that played the Men. They had to bat and bowl left handed. We used to massacre them! We also had our own dances at a hall in Stafford Street. Later, about 1950, we formed a Drama group which went with a bang. If all the Co-op employees came, and brought people with them, we could guarantee full houses for three nights.

Being in the Cash Office we operated a credit system and a lot of people liked to pay the money they owed out of the dividend. Twice a year the whole area of our three offices was geared up for paying out the "Divi".(Only the Wages Office was exempt from the fiasco.) As the customers collected their divi one of us had to rush to the counter and say how much was owed. Some times there was a dispute, some just paid up without a fuss. The whole thing was hectic - it was mad! And by Saturday we knew we had done a week's work. Even the lift would spend the week going up and down like crazy and often used to break down in Dividend Week!

One day it was decided to move the offices to the Stafford Street building. I lost my office and the "wind machine" that I loved so much. There was no Central Cash Department once we moved there, so I moved to Accounts and took over running that. Moving to Stafford Street also caused a split in the staff - separating office staff from shop staff, and our social life was never quite the same again.

The Doorman surveys the scene at the ABC Stourbridge in 1946, while still known as the Savoy. The cinema opened on 11 October 1920 and closed on 6 November 1982. (Author's collection)

Working in the dark

Bernadette Elwell

I started work at the ABC cinema, Stourbridge, back in the sixties. I am a handicapped person, now registered blind, but in those days I was not registered. I had had a lot of trouble with my sight and I had been unemployed for some time. Miss Jones, at the old Labour Exchange, had sent me after all sorts of things, but nobody was interested in me. The one Friday night I was told to go along on Saturday morning for an interview at the cinema.

Mr. Johnson, who was then manager, was away for a few days, so his assistant, Mr. Cook, gave me the job. It was supposed to be a full time job but he was a bit scared that I would be hopeless and that he had done the wrong thing in employing me at all, so he simply gave me a part-time job at first, which would have made it easier with Mr. Johnson if he had done the wrong thing.

I was there for nearly six years. I did the normal usherette's duties which were taking the tickets and showing people to their seats.(But I did far more tearing tickets than showing to seats.) Because I was the youngest I was often sent out on messages and other odd jobs. Mr. Johnson decided that I wasn't capable of carrying the ice-cream tray and he thought I would lose a lot of money in the dark so that's one job he didn't give me. One reason I didn't often have to show people to their seats was that the cinema was seldom that full. If it was full we would have two usherettes working - each taking one side of the cinema.

I had been there for about two years when they decided to put me in the foyer selling the *Film Reviews*, and I was quite successful at that, and I was happy to be talking to people. For the first time I met patrons going into the circle, because up until then I had only met patrons bound for the stalls. With a bit of luck we earned commission on selling the *Film Reviews* - but the system was very unfair. The commission was only paid if they all sold out from all the cinemas in the country. Even if we sold all ours and some unsold ones from another ABC cinema, if one cinema in the country failed to sell out - then none of us received commission! You could work hard, even selling unsold copies from other cinemas, but earn not a penny of commission.

When I started we wore red overalls, and then it was changed to a skirt, blouse and a jacket with ABC on it. We also had little bibs, but they wore out very quickly. I worked six nights a week and Friday was my night off, but I had to go in on Friday to collect my wages. I could have waited until Saturday but, as the money didn't go very far, I was always desperate by Friday.

The people I worked with were quite interesting. Dorothy who worked in the cash desk was a very kind lady, but a little nervous. She used to worry even if she had cashed up correctly. Sometimes when it was right she would worry until she made it wrong! Jake

(Miss Jacobs) used to work in the kiosk. The assistant manager sometimes used to delight in trying to make a fool of me. For instance, once the doorman, Les Grainger, came up to me saying,
"The assistant manager says you've got to help me clean out the boiler!"
I said, "Don't be ridiculous. That's not my job, but if I've got to do it, first you'll have to find someone to look after the tickets for me."
Half an hour later I was hauled into the office and asked why I hadn't gone to clean the boiler? When I said that it wasn't my job and therefore I thought it was a joke, I was then told off for not coming to the office to check!

We had several regulars. One man always brought in a bag of raw peas and sat in the same seat to eat them. One chap talked to himself so much that he drove everyone mad. There was a beautiful lady who came in every Saturday night with her boyfriend. Every week she wore a different suit and always a matching scarf, always so smart, and the suits were so similar, but she must have had at least fifteen, all in a different colour.

I used to think most of the films were rubbish, but some of the rubbish I actually enjoyed. To my shame I liked Vincent Price. One film that I thought was gorgeous was "The Sandpiper", but I never got carried away by the films because I saw them all so many times. Eventually the cinema had to cut back on staff and Head Office insisted that usherettes had to be able to carry ice-cream trays, so I had to leave. I was made redundant. But leaving was one of the best things that ever happened to me. With one week's money, some holiday pay and some money from the Cinema Benevolent Fund, I left with about a hundred pounds in my pocket. I felt rich!

Fred Onions stands at the door of his shop in June 1989, fifty years after establishing the boot and shoe repair business in the front room of his home. (Photo: Ned Williams)

Boot and Shoe Repairs

Fred Onions

As a lad I lived in New Invention and went to school there. My Uncle Harold was the boot repairer in New Invention, so when I came out of school I used to go over and help him to do the finishing with an old rasp and a piece of glass. We had no machinery - everything was done by hand. In that way I picked up the trade generally and, by the time I left school I had a good smattering of it all - how to strip shoes down, how to build heels up and build the soles up. I really got into it and when I left school I would have liked to have gone boot repairing but there was no work about. Uncle Harold could not find me a job so I went into the lock industry. I stayed in the lock industry from the age of fourteen until I was twentyone and then came the great 1929 Depression and I could not get a job anywhere.

I was originally picking up 7/6 off the Labour (37½p), but after six months I went in front of a tribunal and the pay was reduced to 5/- (25p). After another three months, by which time I was twentytwo, they reduced it to 2/6 a week (12½p). I looked around and found nothing doing. The prospects looked very grim so I asked my Uncle if I could collect some shoe repairs on my own would I be able to repair them at his shop. He said I could.

In Coltham Road, Short Heath, I had an Uncle who was a greengrocer so I begged an onion bag off him, got a cycle, and went round collecting boot and shoe repairs. It was tough going because no one in Short Heath knew me as a boot repairer. They couldn't afford to have shoes repaired unless they were going to be done properly, so it was an uphill struggle until I won their confidence. However, I slowly built up a round, collecting and delivering shoes around Short Heath and Lane Head.

My first week's wages was 15/- (75p) - but that was better than 2/6. The following week I earned 18/- and for the next year or so I drew £1 a week from what the business earned and put a bit to one side to build up the business. In 1939 the Ministry of Labour directed me to open a shop in Short Heath. I had been married about twelve months and opened the shop in the front room in our home in Coltham Road - and I've been here ever since.

While I had worked in my Uncle's shop doing my own repairs he had still been a good teacher to me and I had gained a great deal of useful experience. I had no machinery in Coltham Road, but my Uncle gave me an old stitching machine - which I still have, although it must be more than a hundred years old. The first little machine I bought was a finishing machine which cost me £6, and I later bought another machine which was a very good one off a fellow who was retiring. In 1946 it cost me £18 - and I'm still using it today.

Trade prospered during the War when shoes were on ration. It was difficult to buy new shoes so people had to have them repaired - the only drawback was that leather was rationed as well but man made materials and rubber soles and heels were coming in. It was a struggle with prices. To sole and heel mens' shoes was 3/6 (17½p), ladies' shoes were 2/6 (12½p). Mens' heels were 1/3 (7p) and ladies' heels were 9d

(4p). It's never really been a lucrative job. I've been able to live but there was never enough margin in it to make any money, and it's always been a trade that has fluctuated with the seasons and the economic situation.

Over the last few years there has been a lot of disposable footwear and people throw shoes away rather than have them repaired. The trade has declined and a lot of people have left it. At present it just ticks over. I have not retired. I am eighty one but I keep on working a couple of hours every morning to keep myself active and occupied. I like the company in the shop because people come in and out and have a chat even if they are not bringing repairs, and that makes life interesting. Of course, I enjoy the work - I have always loved boot and shoe repairs.

It is difficult to say why I love the trade, apart from the fact that the love does provide incentive and motivation. I like to feel a good shoe, and I like to do a good job and look at the completed article - I get a kick from that - it gives me satisfaction. Boot and shoe repair has never been a drudgery; it's been worthwhile and the end product justifies the labour that is put into it. I am very conscious of shoes, and I do look at peoples' shoes when I'm out.

In the days after the War we had such good solid leather shoes. I used to cut the soles and heels out of the bends (hides) of leather which were hanging on the wall, having been purchased from the tannery in Walsall. I stripped the shoes, cut a pattern, worked the pattern into the bends, marked it and numbered it and cut out the soles and heels. Then they were dropped in the water bosh overnight to soften up - ready to work on the next morning. Today the soles and heels are all cut out for you and the texture is such that I wouldn't like to risk putting a pair in the bosh, because by next next morning they would be like a piece of rag!

Most of our work today is cemented - the soles are cemented in place. The leather of today (they call it "flex") of such a texture that it responds to strong adhesives. You put a layer of cement on the sole and a layer on the shoe and let it go off - it dies completely. It is revived by a little electric activating machine, and then you can make the bond and complete the job.

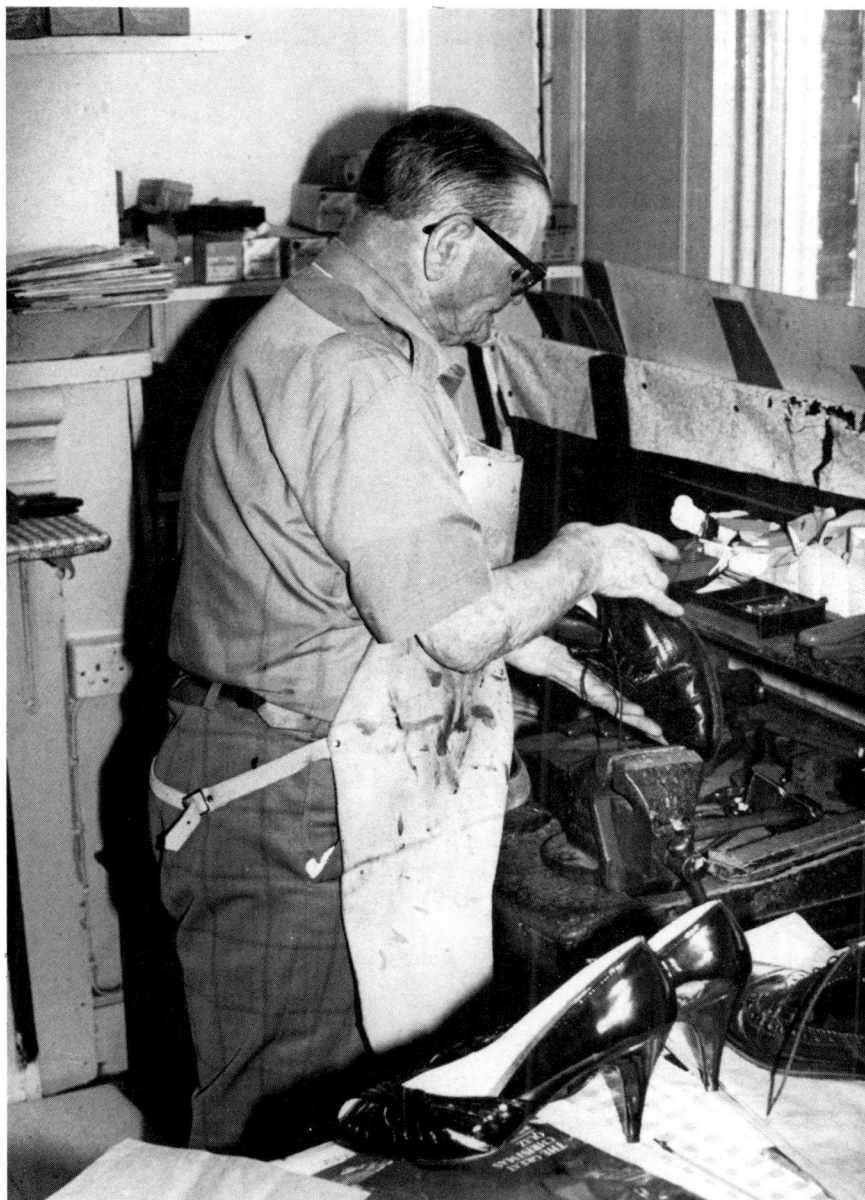

Fred Onions repairing shoes in Coltham Road, Short Heath in June 1989. (Photo: Ned Williams)

In the old days we used nails which had to be held in the mouth. A good boot and shoe repairer can throw the nails into his mouth and almost spit them out into the shoes. Children used to love to watch that part of the job. You have the driver (hammer) in one hand, a stirrup over the shoe to hold it and you fetch the nails out of your mouth and knock them in. As repairers we learnt to speak with a mouth full of nails, and if fifty years I have only swallowed two nails.

I used to have a lot of trade with the miners - the men from Hilton Main, Holly Bank, Allens Rough and the little dog pits. It was very hard work and they always wanted them back the same day, because they couldn't afford two pairs of boots on their wages. They dropped them in on their way home from work. They were always in bad shape and were wet through. They had to be built up and have the hob nails put in - ready to be fetched back at the end of the evening, ready for work the next day.

I was a member of the Wolverhampton Boot & Shoe Repairers Association, and we we met once a month on a Thursday afternoon to exchange ideas. This was very useful as new materials came in. For example, we had a chap from Bilston who invented his own sole-cementing bed, and the Association could buy some items in bulk to sell to members. Naturally I prefer leather to man made materials. There are more corns, bunions and foot ailments about today than there has ever been because these man made materials do not allow the foot to sweat naturally. Leather breathes and absorbs perspiration. The ideal thing is leather throughout.

Just after the War a good class of shoe would cost you 12/6 (62½p). I used to reccommend Lota shoes or Bakers of Wolverhampton but nowadays leather has become even more expensive. A few months ago I repaired a pair of Churchman shoes which cost £103 - but of course they would last forever providing they are regularly repaired and they would be very comfortable. A woman came in the other day with a very awkward job - her shoes had come unstitched all over - they had fallen to pieces, and I told her they would be very difficult to repair, but she said:
"I wish you could do a bit of something with them - You see, I only want to wear them". The funny thing is that if you are really in love with a job - the more difficult it is, the more incentive you can generate to get it done, and if I'm going to do a job, I like it done so that people can look at it and respect the work.

Black Country Folk at work - but not in the Black Country. These hop pickers at Tenbury Wells have all come out to the hop fields for two weeks work, and they all come from Wednesbury. Their photographs were taken and were sold to them as postcards to send back to the rest of the family in Wednesbury. If you have memories of hop picking or even agricultural work within the borders of the Black Country perhaps you would like to contribute them to Volume Two! (Photo: Edna Vaughan's collection)